2017

WOMEN HEROES OF WORLD WAR II

— ★ —

THE PACIFIC THEATER

15 STORIES OF RESISTANCE, RESCUE, SABOTAGE, AND SURVIVAL

Kathryn J. Atwood

CHICAGO
REVIEW
PRESS

Copyright © 2017 by Kathryn J. Atwood
All rights reserved
Published by Chicago Review Press Incorporated
814 North Franklin Street
Chicago, Illinois 60610
ISBN 978-1-61373-168-0

Library of Congress Cataloging-in-Publication Data
Names: Atwood, Kathryn J.
Title: Women heroes of World War II : the Pacific Theater : 15 stories of
   resistance, rescue, sabotage, and survival / Kathryn J. Atwood.
Description: Chicago, Illinois : Chicago Review Press Incorporated, [2016] |
   Includes bibliographical references and index.
Identifiers: LCCN 2016002794| ISBN 9781613731680 (cloth : alk. paper) | ISBN
   9781613731710 (epub) | ISBN 9781613731697 (Kindle)
Subjects: LCSH: World War, 1939-1945—Women—Biography—Juvenile
literature.
   | World War, 1939–1945—Participation, Female—Juvenile literature. |
   World War, 1939–1945—Pacific Area—Juvenile literature. | World War,
   1939–1945—Underground movements—Juvenile literature.
Classification: LCC D810.W7 A86 2016 | DDC 940.53092/525—dc23 LC record
available at http://lccn.loc.gov/2016002794

Image of Claire Phillips on page 89 from *Manila Espionage* by Claire Phillips
and Myron B. Goldsmith; image of Yay Panlilio and Marcos Marking on page
78 from *The Crucible* by Yay Panlilio. Every effort has been made to contact the
copyright holders. The editors would welcome information concerning any
inadvertent errors or omissions.

Interior design: Sarah Olson
Map design: Chris Erichsen
Printed in the United States of America
5 4 3 2 1

To the memory of the courageous
Philippine resistance.

War can teach you so much
about evil, and so much about good.
—ZAINAB SALBI

Heroism is endurance for
one moment more.
—GEORGE F. KENNAN

CONTENTS

AUTHOR'S NOTE

MANY WOMEN IN this book became heroes in the midst of horrific situations. Although I've made every effort to prevent the following stories from being too graphic, readers first encountering the Nanking Massacre, the sufferings of "comfort women," or the brutality of the Kempeitai might be disturbed by certain chapters in this book. I strongly advise younger teens to seek the guidance of a trusted adult.

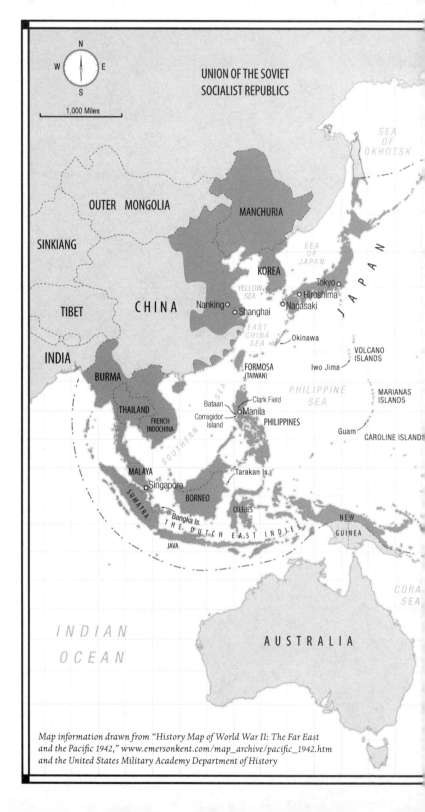

Map information drawn from "History Map of World War II: The Far East and the Pacific 1942," www.emersonkent.com/map_archive/pacific_1942.htm and the United States Military Academy Department of History

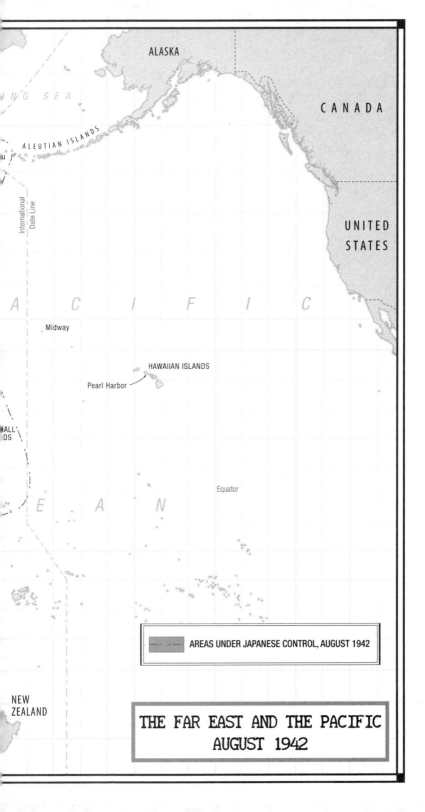

ALASKA

CANADA

ING SEA

ALEUTIAN ISLANDS

International Date Line

UNITED STATES

A   C   I   F   I   C

Midway

HAWAIIAN ISLANDS

Pearl Harbor

ALL DS

Equator

E   A   N

AREAS UNDER JAPANESE CONTROL, AUGUST 1942

NEW ZEALAND

THE FAR EAST AND THE PACIFIC
AUGUST 1942

INTRODUCTION

WHEN DID THE PACIFIC War begin? The first Sunday of December 1941, when the Empire of Japan conducted a series of coordinated, surprise attacks in the Far East? Or was it 1937, when Japan initiated its eight-year war with China? Or earlier still, in 1931, when Japan invaded Manchuria, China's great northeastern province?

These are certainly all major events in World War II's Asia-Pacific time line. But the roots of the war stretch back even further, all the way to the mid-19th century when Japan was an isolated, almost medieval nation, living much the same way it had for centuries.

Japan received a shock on July 8, 1853, when an American commodore named Matthew Perry sailed a group of warships into Tokyo Bay. On a mission from US president Millard Fillmore, Perry pressured the Japanese government to sign several agreements designed to increase trade between Japan and the United States.

Japan had little choice. Some of its leaders insisted on immediate vengeance: a declaration of war on the United States. Others suggested Japan learn from Western nations, then retaliate when they could meet them as equals.

Japan decided on the second option. They sent their best students to Western universities, where they gained valuable knowledge on how to modernize the country. The result was transformation: within three decades Japan had a parliamentary system, industries that exported goods throughout the world, and 6,000 miles of railroad tracks. Its military was also modernized; the Japanese army received instruction from the Germans, and its navy from the British.

But when the Japanese used this new military to seize Far Eastern territory, Western nations tried to discourage them. This seemed extremely hypocritical to Japan: these nations had colonized much of the Far East. Why were they uncomfortable when Japan tried to do the same?

World War I and the Paris Peace Conference

Still, Japan fought on the West's side during World War I. At the postwar Paris Peace Conference, Japan was rewarded for its loyalty with Chinese territory previously controlled by now defeated Germany.

Japan appreciated the gift but was deeply offended by one incident at the conference: the Western nations refused to sign Japan's Racial Equality Proposal, which would have granted the Japanese equality to the Westerners within the League of Nations. Why? Too many Western nations considered all Asians racially inferior; they wouldn't make an exception for their ally.

Then Japan was pressured to sign a series of treaties with the United States and other nations interested in Far Eastern territory. These agreements severely limited the size of the Japanese navy—especially when compared to the navies of the United States and Great Britain—and made Japan promise to honor China's borders.

Japan had been hoping to expand into China in order to offset its own sinking postwar economy—made worse by the worldwide Great Depression of 1929—and to provide extra living space for a postwar population boom. How could Japan fulfill its growing sense of being Asia's greatest nation if it couldn't provide adequately for its own citizens?

The Rise of Fascist Japan

The Japanese began to rethink their association with the West. They searched their own history for answers to their current problems. Before Matthew Perry had sailed into Tokyo Bay, they had lived within a strict feudal social system. The samurai warrior nobles had been at the top.

As the Japanese developed an increasing nostalgia for the once powerful samurai, a group of Japanese military extremists took center stage. While unemployment and political confusion raged, these militarists assassinated prominent politicians in a series of attempted coups. The perpetrators were usually punished, some even executed. Yet they also won the admiration of many Japanese people, gained power, and gradually transformed Japan into a single-party, fascist state, intolerant of opposing political views. The Communist Party was outlawed, and Communists who refused to recant were imprisoned or killed.

The new educational system prepared students for their roles in the emerging nation. Girls were prepared for marriage and motherhood, while boys received premilitary instruction: they learned how to use weapons and were lectured on Japan's racial and cultural superiority and its destiny to rule over the Far East.

Once these young men finished school and entered their required period of military training, they found it differed from that of the samurai in one major point: the military was now a place of equal opportunity. The sons of poor men could rise as quickly as the rich, but only if they survived the first year of what was always brutal training. Random and excessive beatings ensured the trainees—those who were not killed or driven to suicide—emerged as cruel but effective weapons of war, willing to obey any command.

Only one Western ideal now remained at the forefront of the Japanese government: seizing another nation's territory was a sure way toward economic prosperity.

Japan and China

A major cause of Japan's political chaos in the 1930s was its army's controversial seizure of Manchuria, China's large northeastern province.

Even during Japan's 19th-century Westernization, it viewed the once great China in the same way European nations had for decades: as a tool for their own gain. All these nations wanted—by way of forced trade agreements and territorial seizures—a slice of what they called "the Chinese melon." China, ruled from the top by an ancient and corrupt dynasty, and locally by equally corrupt regional warlords in constant strife, was powerless to stop these external assaults.

But in 1911, China threw off its centuries-old dynastic rule through a revolution led by physician-turned-political-leader Sun Yat-sen, who became the first president of the new Republic of China. His eventual successor was Generalissimo Chiang

Kai-shek, who set up a government in Nanking in 1928, claiming that he and his party, the Chinese Nationalists, now controlled all of China. Although this wasn't true—most of the nation was still run by local war lords in an uneasy alliance with the generalissimo—Chiang's talk of Chinese unity troubled the Japanese, who planned to continue their seizure of Chinese territory.

In 1931, they did so in a big way: the Japanese army invaded Manchuria, claiming they were there to quell a disturbance they had secretly created themselves. The Japanese army was there to stay, and Manchuria became a Japanese colony—renamed Manchukuo, Japanese for "Country of the Manchus." Japanese people moved there by the thousands, causing great resentment among the Chinese people.

Chiang, realizing his army was not nearly strong enough to challenge this invasion, endured criticism—especially from the growing and armed Chinese Communists—but he secretly prepared his army for an eventual showdown with Japan.

In December 1936, the Nationalists and the Communists (led by Mao Zedong)—now vying for control of China—put aside their differences in order to defeat their common enemy.

Japan, alarmed by this sudden unity, fearing it might cause trouble in Manchuria, and desiring still more Chinese territory, knew it was time to strike quickly before their enemy became too strong.

On July 7, 1937, Japanese and Chinese soldiers exchanged fire in a northern Chinese village that housed a famous landmark: the Marco Polo Bridge. The Japanese were determined to fan the Marco Polo Bridge incident into a flame. The Chinese were just as determined to take a stand and resist. Hostilities in this full-scale (but never officially declared) war soon began in earnest.

Certain it could conquer all of China, the Japanese army invaded as much of the enormous country it as it could reach.

Western journalists, such as Theodore H. White, who arrived in China in 1939 and became aware of the sad state of most of the Chinese troops, were amazed Japan couldn't win this war. But China seemed to devour the more than one million Japanese troops sent to defeat it. By 1941, approximately 300,000 Japanese fighting men had been killed in China. Yet victory was nowhere in sight; no matter how much territory Japan overran, Chiang Kai-shek refused to surrender. And now other nations threatened to stand in Japan's way.

Many in the United States, including President Franklin Roosevelt, became increasingly horrified by reports of Japanese atrocities against Chinese civilians. Starting in 1938, he initiated a series of economic sanctions against Japan designed to pressure it to end its war with China.

The Lords of the Far East

Japan responded to these sanctions with more aggression. Its leaders seized the opportunity provided by Adolf Hitler's military conquest of much of Europe, including the defeat of France. Without resistance from the new profascist French puppet government, Japanese forces occupied French Indochina a few months later before signing the Tripartite Pact, an agreement with Nazi Germany and Fascist Italy that was a deliberate warning to the then neutral United States to remain so: in addition to granting Japan "lordship" over the Far East, each nation involved in the Pact promised to help the other in case any were attacked by a nation not currently in the war.

During the following summer, the United States cut off all trade with Japan, including an embargo on much-needed oil. Great Britain and the Netherlands then did the same.

With no intention of backing down, the Japanese government decided to get its materials elsewhere—by force. Some of the colonies in the Far East—British Malaya and the Dutch East Indies, especially—were rich in natural resources. If the Japanese could imitate Hitler's example of conquest, they could help themselves to the rubber in Malaya and the oil in the Dutch East Indies.

On the first Sunday of December in 1941—December 7 on one side of the International Date Line, December 8 on the other—Japanese planes bombed the US Navy stationed at Pearl Harbor in Hawaii; the US Air Force stationed in the Philippines; the British fortress at Singapore; the Dutch East Indies; and multiple other locations. These were all surprise attacks; Japan had not officially declared war on any of the nations who controlled these territories. In fact, the Japanese ambassador to the United States was in Washington, DC, discussing Japanese-US relations when the Japanese bombs hit Hawaii.

In Japan this new aggression was greeted with public enthusiasm. The war with China had dragged on for four long years. Suddenly, on a single day, their military had scored not one but multiple victories, transforming the national depression into euphoria. The Japanese people eagerly awaited news of complete victory over the Western imperialists in the Far East. However, many of them, knowing it was dangerously unpatriotic to voice their doubts, wondered silently how many more Japanese men would have to die before this war was won.

But for the present, Japan seemed unstoppable. Their motivation, they claimed, was to implement their idea for a Greater East Asia Co-Prosperity Sphere, "Asia for Asians": defeating the Westerners in order to return control of the Far East to the people who had lived there first. Many Asians (the Chinese excluded, of course) initially believed Japan had their best interests at heart. Western domination of the Far East was based on the racist principle of Caucasian superiority. Surely the Japanese, their fellow Asians, were there to liberate them.

It became immediately obvious this had never been Japan's intention. The Japanese were just as racist toward their fellow Asians as the Westerners before them, and far more cruel. The Japanese government forced hundreds of thousands of civilians into slavery: men into manual labor and women into sexual slavery. Others became the subjects of horrific, secret medical experiments. Then the conquerors plundered all natural resources for themselves.

The Japanese were also unusually cruel to their prisoners of war. The Western military men who had been stationed in the Far East to guard their nation's colonies were shocked to find themselves defeated by an enemy to whom they had once felt superior. They were horrified to discover the Japanese had no intention of honoring the Geneva Convention's code for humane treatment of prisoners of war (POWs); while a representative of the Japanese government had signed it, it had never been officially ratified in Tokyo, Japan's capital city. And because Japanese soldiers were ordered to fight to the death no matter what the circumstances, they had no respect for any military man who laid down his weapon and expected mercy.

The brutal Japanese occupation initiated another war in the Far East, a secret one. Some occupied Asian nations contained large areas of jungle where young men banded into "guerrilla" units (groups of soldiers not part of a regular military) in order to fight the Japanese and their local collaborators by surprise raids, assassinations, and any type of harassment they could manage.

Anyone caught assisting these fighters faced arrest and interrogation by the dreaded Kempeitai, the Japanese military police, who were stationed throughout the conquered Far East. Their gruesome methods for gaining information from anyone suspected of resistance became legendary.

Heroes of the Asia-Pacific War

The women featured in this book are Asians whose nations were invaded by the Japanese or non-Asians who, for one reason or another, found themselves in the Far East during the war. Few of them had previous experience in, or specific training for, the particular circumstances into which the war plunged them. Yet they rose to the challenge: some rescued victims of Japanese aggression; others nursed the wounded in the midst of combat; some created networks to secretly feed starving POWs; others endured torture instead of betraying their fellow resisters; and still others simply survived in desperate circumstances while inspiring those around them to do the same.

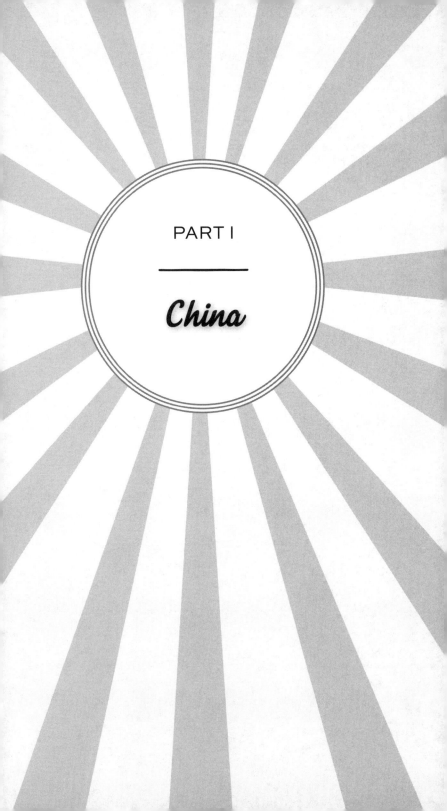

PART I

China

PEGGY HULL

In a War Zone

AMERICAN REPORTER PEGGY Hull was in the midst of a war zone. The lines of this brief battle between Japan and China were not clear: the armies fought wherever and whenever they met, and "the hapless civilian who was caught between them," Peggy wrote, "could expect the fate of a soldier."

Peggy and Sasha, her hired Russian driver, were on their way to interview a Chinese general. As they drove toward his headquarters, they were suddenly trapped: the Chinese were retreating. The Japanese were advancing. Shells were flying toward Peggy and Sasha from both directions as their car raced along a bumpy road.

They noticed a small structure in a nearby field. They abandoned the car and ran to it.

Inside was a coffin and not much else, just the smell of gunfire. Peggy and Sasha tried to catch their breath. Their only hope was that the approaching Japanese had not seen them.

Then, suddenly, another danger appeared, one that was more immediately life-threatening than the exploding shells shaking the walls of the tiny tomb. Would Peggy's life end in a war zone?

She was already an experienced combat reporter. When Mexican bandit-turned-revolutionary Pancho Villa made violent raids near the border of Mexico and the United States, Peggy traveled with US National Guard troops sent to capture him. During World War I, Peggy reported on an American artillery training camp in France. And when Entente troops were sent to support the White Russians during the Siberian Intervention of the Russian Civil War, Peggy went along.

However, she hadn't come to China in 1932 to report on war. She claimed she was now willing to leave that topic to male reporters. Instead, she planned to write articles about Chinese women for female American readers.

But on January 28, 1932, Shanghai, China's large port city, was suddenly a battle zone. Several Japanese monks had been beaten in the streets by Chinese citizens who were angered over the recent Japanese invasion of Manchuria. A Japanese factory was burned down. The Japanese navy, eager to prove itself as battle-worthy as the army had in Manchuria, brought fighting men ashore in Shanghai. A Japanese admiral named Kōichi Shiozawa demanded a formal apology and compensation from Chinese Generalissimo Chiang Kai-shek. Chiang offered a public compromise but privately encouraged his army to fight back. What followed would become known as the Shanghai Incident, the January 28 Incident, or the First Battle of Shanghai.

The *New York Daily News* didn't have a reporter in Shanghai. Peggy was nearby. "Go to work," the editor cabled her. "You're our correspondent."

She found someone with their own shortwave radio who could quickly transmit her stories to the United States. Then

Peggy located an observation post on the top of a flour mill. It was dangerous but she could see the battle.

Peggy Hull aboard a Japanese ship in Shanghai, 1932, with a Japanese admiral named Nomura Kichisaburō. *Kansas Historical Society*

On January 29, 1932, she witnessed the first major Japanese assault:

> In company with other Americans I stood on the roof of the tallest building in the international settlement for three hours watching the planes drop their bombs. With the others I saw the resultant flames destroy hundreds of tenement homes in Chapei, where dwell close to 1,000,000 Chinese laborers. The tenements crumbled like pie crusts and the ruins burst into flames as the terrified Chinese fled into the narrow streets, running in packs like bewildered animals. Thousands huddled in the debris. It was a frightful scene of human misery.

Because the United States was neutral, Peggy was free to move between Chinese and Japanese military bases. She was even invited to have dinner with a Japanese commander stationed in Shanghai, Admiral Nomura Kichisaburo.

★★

MODERNIZING JAPANESE WOMEN

By the 1920s, many Japanese women had become increasingly Western in terms of dress, behavior, and thought. But the military extremists who seized control of the government were determined to change this. In 1932, they produced a propaganda film called *Japan in the National Emergency*. The film officially urged Japanese women to reject Western ideals of equality with men and return to their traditional subservient role.

★★

During the dinner, Admiral Nomura annoyed Peggy when he claimed American men couldn't fight. She was even more annoyed with his explanation: American women were too independent. Japanese women, he claimed, strengthened their men by staying quiet and dependent.

Still, Admiral Nomura liked Peggy and gave her a safe conduct pass: a small, square piece of cloth with a red Japanese symbol in one corner and black Japanese characters on one side. "If you are ever in danger with the Japanese troops," he said, "show this. You are the only foreigner to whom we are giving this type of identification."

A few days later, Peggy arranged an interview with a Chinese officer, General Tsai Ting-Kai, who was considered a hero for his brave defense of Shanghai.

Sasha, the driver she hired to escort her to General Tsai's headquarters, had escaped from the Red Army during the Russian Civil War after being left for dead on a frozen battlefield. After trudging for miles, starved and alone, he finally arrived in China via a caravan. Now he made his living in Shanghai as a tourist chauffeur.

When Sasha again found himself in the middle of a war zone, huddled in the tiny tomb with Peggy, something snapped. He became deeply disturbed. "His body shook," wrote Peggy later, "and I knew that at any moment, at any second, he might break. And I knew that I was responsible for his being here. He would not forget that."

Sasha's body convulsed in synchronization to sounds of shells and bullets, as if he were being hit by each one. All the while, his eyes were fixed on Peggy with an expression of "increasing, deadly resolve."

When his "hands began to twist, his long fingers closing tightly against some imagined object," Peggy sensed that he was going to try to kill her, perhaps out of a crazed desire to cheat death himself.

Peggy knew her slightest movement might send Sasha lunging toward her. But she had to break the spell. Without turning from his gaze, she reached for the door. It opened a crack.

A beam of light fell across Sasha's face. It startled him. He made an odd guttural sound and rushed out of the grave, apparently unaware of his surroundings. He was shot almost immediately.

Overwhelmed with pity at Sasha's ironic fate, Peggy sat down in the grave and pondered her own: "Like Sasha, I had come a long way . . . and now I was caught in a grave—maybe my own."

The Japanese were headed toward the grave; Peggy could see them through the partially open door. To protect themselves from a sniper who might be hiding inside, they fired at the tomb in regular intervals as they approached. Peggy was paralyzed with confusion and indecision. With fear.

The desire to live suddenly overpowered all her other emotions. Peggy swung the door wide open. The rush of air cleared her mind. Then she remembered something that might just save her life: the safe conduct pass from Admiral Nomura!

She fumbled through her bag and found the piece of cloth. She fastened it to her coat, over her heart; that's where the men would take aim, that's where they would look first. Then she fluffed her hair; if the Japanese recognized her gender, it might save her life.

Peggy crawled out of the tomb. She stood up, hands on her head.

The Japanese saw her. Their bayonets gleamed in the sunlight. Peggy knew they were trained killers. But she saw something in their faces that surprised her: fear. "In the briefest period of time," she wrote later, "I realized that all military heroism, all senseless butchery, destruction, and life-letting were only the offsprings of men driven by inhuman fear."

She walked out to meet the lieutenant, pointing to the safe conduct pass. He was clearly astonished. Then he bowed to her. The men dropped their rifles. In perfect English the lieutenant asked, "You are lost?"

He graciously allowed Peggy an escort back to the headquarters of General Yoshinori Shirakawa, a Japanese officer Peggy had met in Siberia in 1919. When she came face-to-face with him, he smiled and said, "You know, if you do not give up your war corresponding, you are surely going to end your life in a battlefield."

The conflict ended on March 3, 1932. By then, 14,000 Chinese people had lost their lives, including 10,000 civilians. On March 4, Peggy filed her last story for the *Daily News*.

One year later, in February 1933, the League of Nations formally condemned Japan for its takeover of Manchuria. Japan responded by leaving the league. The war between China and Japan was just beginning.

When Japan expanded its war with China to include most of the Far East in 1941 and 1942, Peggy couldn't get immediate accreditation to cover the war. Now she had two things against her: not only her gender but also her age. She was 53.

She settled for reporting in Hawaii on wounded men coming in from the Pacific island battles.

"The mangled bodies of boys," Peggy wrote, "who were so young and virile a short time before . . . now mutilated, some beaten for life. . . . It was an agony to see them go; worse to see them come back."

In January 1945, Peggy finally received accreditation to visit the islands in the Pacific. Women correspondents were allowed to land on these islands with or shortly after the military nurses, which often meant that the Japanese were still in the area. While in the Marianas Islands, Peggy was told one morning that a Japanese sniper had been found only 100 yards from her quarters.

During her interviews, Peggy learned that some of the American fighting men were disgusted with the racially inspired

Peggy Hull in 1945. *Kansas Historical Society*

attacks against Japanese Americans in the United States. They were particularly angered by an incident in which a crazed mob forced a Japanese American farmer to leave his employment on a New Jersey farm. "We are not fighting to inherit a world full of hatred and suspicion," the men told Peggy, "and when the people at home stage a scene like that we feel betrayed. Why can't they let us do the fighting out here where it belongs? Sometimes we wonder what we will be going back to."

The fighting men, grateful that Peggy cared enough to listen to their stories, gave her patches from their "outfits"—military divisions—that they wanted her to place on her beret. By the end of the war Peggy had collected 50 such patches, which she displayed on a total of seven berets.

Peggy was not only interested in what the fighting men had to say; she also tried to learn all she could about civilians in previously occupied areas. While reporting from the Marianas Islands, Peggy learned that the locals had been brutalized by the Japanese. "They were sent to the fields to work like slaves," she wrote, "and their food was rationed to them in small, inadequate amounts. They were beaten and beheaded and shot because they did not know the intricate and senseless routine of Japanese manners. They were tortured for information which they did not have."

Peggy hoped to follow the troops all the way to Japan, partly because she wanted to ask Admiral Nomura if he had changed his mind about American men and their ability to wage war. But Japan surrendered before the invasion became necessary.

After the war, Peggy decided to stop working as a war correspondent. Meeting wounded men face-to-face had disturbed her deeply. She no longer considered war an adventure but a tragedy. As the years went on, Peggy felt her work had been forgotten. She became increasingly reclusive: she was ashamed to no longer appear the dashing reporter her friends and family remembered. Two years before her death, she found a measure of peace by joining the Catholic Church.

Peggy died of breast cancer on June 19, 1967, at the age of 76.

LEARN MORE

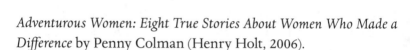

Adventurous Women: Eight True Stories About Women Who Made a Difference by Penny Colman (Henry Holt, 2006).

Eye Witness by Members of the Overseas Press Club of America edited by Robert Spiers Benjamin (Alliance Book Corporation, 1940). The first chapter is Peggy's report, "Open Grave in Shanghai."

"Peggy Hull Deuell: Woman War Correspondent, 1890–1967," Kansas Historical Society, www.kshs.org/kansapedia/peggy-hull-deuell/15137.

Reporting Under Fire: 16 Daring Women War Correspondents and Photojournalists by Kerrie Logan Hollihan (Chicago Review Press, 2014).

The Wars of Peggy Hull: The Life and Times of a War Correspondent by Wilda M. Smith and Eleanor A. Bogart (Texas Western Press, 1991).

MINNIE VAUTRIN

American Hero at the Nanking Massacre

IN DECEMBER 1937, Nanking was a city in flight. Its streets were jammed with the last major flood of civilians who had the means to leave the war-torn city. Half the original population was now gone. Most of the remaining 500,000 civilians were there only because they couldn't afford transportation or had nowhere else to go.

But there was one small group of foreigners in Nanking—Americans and Europeans—who had stayed deliberately. They were the members of the International Committee for the Nanking Safety Zone, which referred to an approximate three-mile area in the city designed to be a wartime refuge for civilians. Women and children were to be housed within the safety zone at Ginling Women's College. Its president was an American woman named Minnie Vautrin.

Educated at the University of Illinois, Minnie had fallen in love with China when she was first sent there by a missionary

"Committee which organized the first religious work among the women and girls at Ginling College," 1938. Minnie Vautrin is pictured front row, center. *Matthew Forster and Michael Forster, Yale Divinity School Library*

society in order to start a school for Chinese girls. Minnie eventually moved on to Ginling Women's College in Nanking.

In July 1937, Minnie was on vacation when she heard that Japanese and Chinese troops had exchanged fire at the Marco Polo Bridge near Peking (Beijing). She rushed back to Nanking, where she found the city preparing for war. In August, war erupted in Shanghai. Nanking would certainly be next. Why? It was Chiang Kai-shek's Nationalist capital and an example of what he wanted all China to be: a perfect blend of ancient culture and modern technology. To destroy it would be an enormous symbolic victory for Japan.

While Minnie and others prepared the campus defensively for war, she discussed other possibilities with some colleagues, summarizing their conversation in her diary: "Are we to stand by hopelessly and see war come upon the Orient or is there something that we can do—and if so, what?"

Minnie certainly did not want to "stand by." She began to drill her students on air raid procedures. One hour later, the Japanese dropped their first bombs on Nanking. The air raids continued almost daily throughout the rest of the summer and autumn, each time killing and wounding hundreds of civilians. Bomb shelters sprang up all over the city, Ginling College included, where Minnie directed their construction.

The courage shown by the Chinese during the air raids gave Minnie a new respect for them: "If Japan only knew it," she wrote in her diary on September 26, "she is welding the Chinese together as a nation more firmly day by day. There is a courage, a confidence, and a determination that I have never seen before. To go along the street and to see the many new [bomb shelters] makes you feel that China is digging in and is determined never to yield but to sacrifice all, if that is necessary."

Toward the end of November, Minnie walked down one of Nanking's main roads. Nearly every store was closed. Military vehicles raced past carrying war supplies and military officers. Mule carts and rickshaws, moving slower, carried fleeing civilians. And Minnie encountered women and children who asked her for the exact location of the safety zone.

Minnie estimated that Ginling could house a total of 2,750 refugees. But by December 11, only 750 had come. That was about to change.

On December 12, orders came for the surviving Chinese army to evacuate by way of the Yangtze River. The Nanking defenders were poorly trained, ill-equipped, and spoke a variety of confusing dialects. And there weren't enough boats for all of them to escape across the river. When the Japanese dropped leaflets from planes promising leniency to anyone who surrendered, the confused, exhausted, stranded Chinese soldiers were all too willing to believe them.

They shouldn't have. The Japanese army was in no mood to be gracious. Their leaders had promised that all of China—populated by a race they considered subhuman—would be defeated within three months. But they had been fighting there for four, and very little of the enormous nation was under their control. The Japanese were ready to avenge themselves, assert their supremacy, and terrify the rest of China into surrendering quickly.

On December 13, the remaining Chinese soldiers outside Nanking meekly surrendered by the thousands. They were machine-gunned to death. The Japanese army now turned its attention to the city.

When the fighting stopped the day before, Minnie took note of the sudden silence in her diary before voicing her main concern: "Our fate at the hands of a victorious army."

Minnie came face-to-face with representatives of that army on December 16 when a group of officers arrived at Ginling to search the campus for any hidden Chinese soldiers. They apparently didn't believe her when she explained the safety zone was a civilian refuge. "They wanted every room opened," wrote Minnie, "and if the key was not forthcoming immediately they were most impatient and one of their party stood ready with an ax to open the door by force." The Japanese set up six machine guns around the campus to shoot any fleeing Chinese soldiers.

While no Chinese soldiers were found at Ginling, they were found elsewhere within the safety zone. John Rabe, a local German businessman, head of the Nazi party in Nanking, and the leader of the safety zone, had earlier encountered 400 starved and straggling Chinese soldiers. Although it was against the rules, Rabe's pity for them was so great, he convinced them to throw away their weapons and seek shelter in the safety zone until they could be arrested. He didn't realize then that all surrendering soldiers would be murdered. When the Japanese discovered them, they took them away, along with hundreds of civilian workers—rickshaw coolies, manual laborers, police officers—accused of being soldiers in disguise because they, like soldiers, had calloused hands.

The Japanese method of prisoner execution began to alter in a gruesome way: prisoners were used in a series of beheading and bayoneting contests, to see which Japanese soldier could first reach 100 kills.

When these contests came to Rabe's attention, he complained repeatedly and urgently to the officials at the Japanese embassy. But the embassy was powerless to stop the grisly murders. Deeply frustrated, Rabe decided to drive out alone into the city to see if he could prevent crimes from occurring there. He was immediately besieged by frantic Chinese men who pleaded with him to save their female relatives from being raped by Japanese soldiers.

Rabe had nothing with which to deter the soldiers except his swastika armband. That symbol, along with his reckless courage, intimidated a surprising number of Japanese rapists who fled when he confronted them.

But he couldn't stop them all. No female in Nanking was safe: elderly women were raped along with girls under the age of 10. The victims were often killed immediately afterward, and their naked corpses filled streets lined with posters that read, "Trust Our Japanese Army: They Will Protect and Feed You."

As the atrocities mounted outside the gates of the safety zone, horrified civilian refugees flooded through them. Minnie, keeping watch at Ginling's gates, encountered "a stream of

★★

PEER PRESSURE AND THE JAPANESE SOLDIERS IN NANKING

Not all Japanese soldiers were initially eager to participate in Nanking's atrocities. One of them stated the following during a postwar interview:

> Our officers told us we could kill and rape as many of "the Chinese enemy" as we pleased. There were some of us however, who did not like the idea, including myself. When we did not join the others in shooting and bayoneting the civilians, we were ridiculed and made fun of. Our troops were holding competitions among themselves to see who could shoot or bayonet to death the most Chinese within a specific time. Eventually, I was persuaded to join them. A sergeant told me with a laugh, "Killing a Chinese is just like killing a dog! You'll feel nothing!"

After killing his first victim, the young man admitted to killing "many Chinese of all ages, even children. I did not feel any remorse."

★★

weary wild-eyed women [who] said their night had been one of horror; that again and again their homes had been visited by [Japanese] soldiers."

Still claiming to be searching for Chinese soldiers, the Japanese now entered Ginling to rape and loot. When Minnie insisted on accompanying them, they tried to outwit her by entering the campus in different groups, staggered throughout the day. Surely this American woman couldn't accompany them all.

She couldn't. But that didn't stop her from trying. Minnie spent most of her time running from one end of the campus to another, trying to stay one step ahead of the raping, looting soldiers. Her commanding presence was enough to make some of them quit, but others, she wrote, would look at her "with a dagger in their eyes and some times a dagger in their hands." One Japanese soldier became so angry with Minnie when she tried to prevent a looting, he pointed a gun at her. Another slapped her.

Meanwhile, the refugees continued to flood into Ginling, "with horror written on their faces," wrote Minnie, and relating "stories of tragedies such as I have never heard before."

Minnie was desperate. She decided to visit the Japanese embassy in Nanking to see if anyone there would help her.

A sympathetic embassy clerk wrote two official letters ordering the soldiers to leave the women of Ginling alone. He also gave Minnie some official "proclamations" to post on the outside of Ginling's walls, declaring the campus off-limits to Japanese soldiers.

He even arranged for Minnie to be driven home in the embassy car. The driver told Minnie, "the only thing that had saved the Chinese people from utter destruction" were the "handful of foreigners" running Nanking's safety zone. Minnie was glad to be making a difference, of course, but the driver's words filled her with a certain despair: "What would it be like," she wrote, "if there were no check on this terrible devastation and cruelty?"

On the following day, she tested the power of the letters. While racing from one end of the campus to the other, as usual, Minnie was told that two Japanese soldiers had taken a girl into

a room and were no doubt in the process of raping her. Storm-
ing inside to challenge them, Minnie presented them with the
embassy letter. They fled. Describing the incident in her diary
that night, Minnie made it clear she wished to do more: "In my
wrath I wished I had the power to smite them in their dastardly
work."

But the letters weren't always so effective. A Japanese soldier
ripped one to shreds in Minnie's face. Others tore the proclamations off of Ginling's walls. And Minnie still spent most of
her day attempting to outrun groups of Japanese soldiers. But
because some were intimidated by the documents, Minnie
was determined to keep posting them. She visited the Japanese
embassy continuously to obtain replacements.

Some Chinese people now began wearing armbands that
displayed the rising sun emblem of the Japanese flag, hoping
this would offer them some protection. Minnie would not allow
anyone wearing one to enter Ginling. She removed the band
from the arm of one young Chinese man visiting his sister at
Ginling, telling him, "There is no need for you to wear this rising sun emblem. You are a Chinese, your country has not per-
ished." She would often encourage her staff in a similar way,
assuring them that "the Japanese will definitely fail at the end."

Toward the end of December, there were approximately
10,000 women and children crammed into Ginling. In what
time she could spare, Minnie helped supervise their lives. The
Red Cross set up a rice kitchen near the front gate. At first, the
desperate women fought with each other for a place in line. But
Minnie directed two of her associates to help them wait in an
orderly manner.

On January 28, the Japanese army ordered all camps in the
safety zone to be closed by February 4. They claimed it was now
safe for everyone to return to their homes.

It wasn't. When some women, trusting the Japanese promises, went home and were raped, the survivors fled back to Ginling, begging Minnie to allow them to stay. Minnie believed their stories and agreed to let them back in. "Women do not willingly tell me these tales," she wrote, "for they feel the disgrace of it too deeply."

On the day of the deadline, February 4, two policemen from the Japanese embassy came to announce that Ginling's refugee camp was to be shut down. When they entered Ginling, Minnie faced them. She told them that those remaining were from areas too far away or had no way to make a living without their missing male relatives. She would not make them leave.

The grateful Ginling refugees gave Minnie new nicknames: Living Goddess and Goddess of Mercy.

But Minnie wasn't a goddess. She was a human being deeply shaken by what she had seen. On February 8, 1938, she and John Rabe attended a military band concert at the Japanese embassy; they had responded to the invitation out of sense of duty. The military music conjured up horrific images for Minnie:

When they played the overture "Light Cavalry," my mind would not leave that procession that passed our gate on December 14—that group of one hundred or more civilians with bound hands, walking behind the Japanese soldiers and cavalry—the group that has never returned; and when they proudly played "Our Army," the destroyed cities, desolate country side, raped women and girls, kept ever before me—I don't think I heard the music.

Although haunted by memories and her strength ebbing dangerously, Minnie didn't take the time to stop and rest. There was too much to do. Hundreds of young women in Ginling begged her to help them find their missing husbands, all of them civilians. Minnie tried to locate the men through the Japanese embassy, but they had little information; it was assumed they were all dead. Because most had been the only source of their family's income, Minnie decided to begin training classes at Ginling that would enable new widows to gain skills with which to support their families.

On July 30, 1938, the Chinese Nationalist government quietly awarded Minnie with the Order of the Jade, the highest honor possible for any foreigner in China. It was secretly delivered to the American embassy in Nanking on January 23, 1939.

While the most blatant atrocities had now passed, the continued occupation of Nanking was deeply oppressive. The Japanese opened up narcotics dens that turned masses of desperate Nanking citizens into addicts and thieves. Thousands also became the subjects of ghastly, secret medical experiments. The city's economy was shattered; prices on basic necessities became sky-high. At one point Minnie had to ask campus workers to cut down trees for fuel. Her office was always bitterly cold. Yet she was determined to stay in Nanking, turning down two very prestigious offers of work in the United States in order to do so.

But by the spring of 1940, Minnie finally had to acknowledge her strength was gone. After being examined by a doctor, it was clear she had suffered a complete physical and emotional breakdown that would require lengthy treatment and rest in the United States.

This enforced inactivity was extremely difficult for a woman who wanted to be helping, not to be helped. After Nazi Germany attacked Western Europe in the spring of 1940, Minnie wrote the following to a friend: "At a time when the whole world is in such travail and agony, I am sorry to be on the side lines, helpless and a burden."

OUTCOME OF THE NANKING MASSACRE

Although the Japanese government immediately tried to cover up the Nanking Massacre, members of the International Committee for the Nanking Safety Zone exposed it to the world by way of eloquent written testimony, photographs, and even some motion picture film, all of it smuggled out of the city. After the war, several Japanese officers were found guilty of war crimes for their part in the massacre and were executed. Nevertheless, the massacre continues to be a source of tension between China and Japan to this day, and the casualty numbers disputed: the Chinese estimate that between 20,000 to 80,000 women were raped and 300,000 civilians and unarmed POWs murdered. The Japanese estimates are far lower. A surprising number of Japanese people deny that any war crimes occurred there at all.

Haunted, exhausted, and hopeless, Minnie took her own life on May 14, 1941, in Indianapolis, one more casualty of the Nanking Massacre.

LEARN MORE

─────────── ★ ───────────

American Goddess at the Rape of Nanking: The Courage of Minnie Vautrin by Hua-ling Hu (Southern Illinois University Press, 2000).

The Undaunted Women of Nanking: The Wartime Diaries of Minnie Vautrin and Tsen Shui-Fang edited by Hua-ling Hu and Zhang Lian-hong (Southern Illinois University Press, 2010).

GLADYS AYLWARD

"All China Is a Battlefield"

BY THE SPRING OF 1938, the Japanese army had invaded and occupied large sections of northern China. Many of the Chinese soldiers in northern areas not yet occupied by the Japanese were ill-equipped and commanded by warlord generals with various and conflicting levels of loyalty to Nationalist leader Chiang Kai-shek. Communist guerrillas randomly attacked Japanese troops from behind. China, disorganized though it was, fought on in whatever ways it could and refused to surrender.

Japan took the war to China's civilians as they had in Nanking: burning, looting, raping, and killing. By the end of the war, between 80 to 100 million Chinese civilians would become refugees. Many of these refugees were war orphans.

In a bombed-out mission in the northwestern Shanxi province, in the town of Yangcheng, a British-missionary-turned-Chinese-citizen, Gladys Aylward, was caring for more than 100 of these war orphans. Each week children were brought to

Gladys Aylward, shortly before leaving China. The Small Woman *by Alan Burgess (Reprint Society, 1957)*

the mission or wandered in by themselves; anyone who knew Gladys Aylward understood she would never turn away an orphaned child.

Gladys was urged to contact Madame Chiang, wife of Chiang Kai-shek. The generalissimo's wife was opening orphanages in the Shaanxi province, just west of the Shanxi province.

Madame Chiang replied quickly to Gladys's letter. "If you can bring the children into Free China to Shaanxi," she wrote, "we will look after them."

Soon 100 children were on their way with one of Gladys's trusted friends. But before a month had passed, 100 more orphans had found their way to the mission.

One day, a Chinese general sent Gladys a message: the Japanese were approaching Yangcheng in large numbers. The Chinese army was retreating. He wanted Gladys to come with them. They would care for the children on the way.

Although Gladys was concerned for the children's safety, she rarely feared for her own. The children left with the general and his men. Gladys remained at Yangcheng.

Two nights after their departure, a Chinese soldier knocked on her door, telling Gladys he had been sent back to once more persuade her to leave.

"Whether you leave with us nor not, you must leave. We have received certain information."

"What information?" Gladys asked.

"The Japanese have put a price on your head."

"You are just saying this to make me leave," Gladys replied.

He wasn't. The soldier pulled a paper out of his pocket, one of many, he said, that had been found posted on a nearby city wall. The paper listed three names and stated the following: "Any person giving information which will lead to the capture, alive or dead, of the above mentioned, will receive [a large sum of money] from the Japanese High Command." One of the names listed on the poster was "Ai-weh-deh," Gladys's official Chinese name.

Why did this missionary have a price on her head?

She had come to China in 1932 on the Trans-Siberian Railway during an undeclared war between the Soviet Union and

China. After being stopped, nearly attacked, then ordered to work in the Soviet Union, Gladys escaped and completed the trip to Yangcheng—a place where few Europeans had yet ventured—by boat, bus, and mule.

In Yangcheng, Gladys and an elderly Scottish missionary named Jennie Lawson opened a public house they named the Inn of the Eight Happinesses. Here the two women fed and sheltered "muleteers," men who traveled on months-long journeys by mule caravans, transporting goods and equipment throughout the province.

While the muleteers ate, the women told them Bible stories. Because the men enjoyed the stories and because they traveled so widely, the innkeepers' fame spread quickly. Gladys longed to speak the local Chinese dialect as well as Jennie, so she studied hard. After she had been in China for one year—during which time Jennie died of an illness related to old age—Gladys was quite fluent.

Shortly after Jennie's death, Gladys was visited by an important local official, the Mandarin of the Shanxi province. He asked Gladys if she would help him stamp out the practice of foot binding—tightly wrapping the feet of female babies and young girls to give them a permanently hobbled way of walking, then widely considered an important symbol of femininity and crucial for making a good marriage. The province's warlord had ordered the Mandarin to stop foot binding in that part of the Shanxi province, but the Mandarin didn't think it proper work for a man. And Gladys was the only woman in the district who could endure long journeys because she was the only woman in the area with unbound feet.

The Mandarin promised Gladys two soldiers for protection, a mule for traveling, and a small salary. Gladys took up the challenge and traveled to many small villages in the Shanxi province. She always broke the initial tension with stories and songs. Then she gently but firmly explained that the villagers had to stop crippling the feet of their daughters. The alternative was prison.

The villagers sensed Gladys was a kind woman, despite the threatening soldiers accompanying her and the consequences facing them if they didn't cooperate. They often followed her to wherever she stayed for the night and requested more stories. Gladys became known as "the Storyteller."

By 1936, Gladys had been in China for four years. Her language, appearance, and behavior, even her way of thinking, were now more Chinese than British. She decided to become a Chinese citizen. She took the name the Chinese people had already given her: Ai-weh-deh, which means "virtuous woman."

Although she thoroughly enjoyed her work, Gladys was often lonely and longed for a family of her own. One day during her travels, she noticed a woman begging by the roadside in the harsh sunlight. Beside the woman was a small child who was dirty, ill, and covered with sores. Gladys warned the woman that the sick child would die if not taken out of the sun.

"Well, if she does," the woman replied, "I can get another to take her place."

Gladys was horrified: the woman was using the sick child for money. She purchased the girl for five Chinese coins. Because the amount was about the same as ninepence in English money, Gladys named the girl Ninepence. Nineteen more orphans soon found their way into Gladys's home, and she adopted them all. She now had a family.

Then, one spring day in 1938, war came to Yangcheng. The villagers ran out of their homes to a sight they'd never seen before: airplanes. But their excitement quickly turned to terror when those planes began to rain destruction and death all over the town.

The inn was hit in several places. Gladys was knocked unconscious and had to be dug out of the rubble by some neighbors. When she recovered consciousness, she helped transform part of the inn into a first aid station. And despite the danger, she continued to travel from village to village, holding Christian meetings that were usually well attended. Some of the attendees were now Japanese soldiers.

Yangcheng changed hands four times from the Japanese to the Chinese, each battle bringing more destruction and misery to the town. Gladys continued to use what was left of the inn courtyard to nurse the wounded, both Chinese and Japanese.

One day, four Chinese men dressed in civilian clothes came to see Gladys. The leader's name was Linnan. He told Gladys he was working for Chiang Kai-shek's intelligence service.

"Will you help China?" he asked.

"I'm Chinese—naturalized Chinese—and I care deeply about what happens to this country." But, Gladys continued, she hadn't come to China to help it win a war.

Linnan tried to persuade her. "Japanese intentions are evil, are they not? China is fighting to the death in an effort to prevent this evil from spreading."

Gladys thought about this, then gave her answer: "I will help you as far as my conscience will allow me."

The next time she traveled through occupied Japanese territory to hold Christian meetings, she took note of how many Japanese soldiers were in a particular area and what sort of weapons they carried. The Japanese didn't seem to notice her—she looked like another ordinary war refugee. So she passed back and forth through their lines unsuspected, sometimes leading Nationalist troops right into Japanese positions.

As she provided information to Linnan, her patriotism grew, as did her desire to work against the Japanese, who, she would write later, "had despoiled our country, disturbed our way of life and killed our friends."

Now Gladys had discovered that the Japanese wanted to kill her and were offering a reward for her capture. The Chinese soldier who had been sent to urge her to flee for her own safety awaited her answer.

Gladys was torn by her sense of responsibility for the area. Perhaps there was a good reason she had received this warning. But she longed for more direction, some sort of sign. She opened her Bible. The first words she saw were these: "Flee ye, flee ye into the mountains." She burned all incriminating documents and pictures and made plans to leave the next day.

But when morning came and her mule was being prepared for travel, a fellow villager gestured to the peephole in the main village gate. "No mule will get out of here today, Ai-weh-deh. They are here; they came last night," he said. When Gladys looked through the peephole, she saw Japanese soldiers washing their feet.

The only other exit out of the town was the Gate of the Dead, the path reserved for removing dead bodies. Gladys got through it, crossed a stream, and was in an open field before the Japanese spotted her.

She heard them shouting. Bullets flew past her head. She dove to the ground, rolled under a bush, ran, fell, ran, hid, crawled, always moving forward, until the firing stopped.

Within two days she found the village of Cheng Tsuen where the first group of children had gone. They were still not safe. Cheng Tsuen was being bombed regularly. Someone needed to take the children to Sian (now Xi'an), capital of the Shaanxi province.

Gladys decided to take them. Her friends in Cheng Tsuen tried to talk her out of it. It was a 200-mile trip, they said, nearly impossible to accomplish with so many small children. And what's more, the Japanese now had control of every road along the way.

But Gladys was determined to get the children to safety. If the roads were too dangerous, she would travel over the mountains.

At first, the children were excited and happy, as if they were on an adventure. They walked along the mountain paths and slept in temples or out in the open, huddling together for warmth.

But after a few days, the younger children became exhausted and tearful. The older children couldn't carry them far before becoming worn out themselves. Gladys tried to distract and energize everyone with songs.

After 12 exhausting days, the great Yellow River—a major milestone on their journey—came into view. They walked down to the riverbank and waited for the expected ferryboat. After hours with no boat in sight, Gladys left the younger children in the care of the older and visited the local military headquarters. They told her the boats were no longer running; they were all on the other side. The Japanese were expected there at any moment, and the Chinese, of course, didn't want to supply their enemy with easy transport across the river.

Gladys returned to the hungry children at the riverbank. She spent a sleepless, despairing night wondering why she had taken on this task, why she had placed them all in this dangerous and impossible situation.

At dawn, one of the older children, Sualan, asked Gladys if she remembered the Bible story about Moses and the children of Israel crossing the Red Sea.

When Gladys nodded, Sualan then asked if she believed it.

"I would not teach you anything I did not believe," said Gladys.

"Then why does not God open the waters of the Yellow River for us to cross?" asked Sualan.

"I'm not Moses, Sualan," Gladys replied.

Sualan reminded her that God hadn't changed. Gladys suddenly wondered if she had ever really believed her own stories, the ones she'd never stopped sharing since she'd come to China. And what could she say now to this trusting young girl?

"Let you and I kneel down and pray, Sualan," said Gladys. "And perhaps soon our prayers will be answered."

A short time later, she heard the children screaming with delight, "Ai-weh-deh, here's a soldier! A soldier!"

A Chinese patrol officer, who had heard the children's voices, approached, clearly surprised to see them. The river was closed, he explained. Japanese planes regularly patrolled this area, shooting at anything that moved.

"This will soon be a battlefield," he continued. Didn't she realize that?

"All China is a battlefield," Gladys replied wearily.

He said he would try to get them a boat. He put his fingers in his mouth and whistled sharply three times. Gladys heard three response whistles from across the river. A boat soon appeared and ferried the children in groups until they were all safely across.

After a few days of rest in a nearby village, Gladys and the children set out for Miechin, where they were to catch a train that would bring them closer to the orphanage in Sian.

But the train stopped prematurely; the Japanese had invaded the area, and they always targeted China's railway system. This train would go no farther.

Gladys was once again stranded. She pleaded with the stationmaster: she had 100 children with her. They had been on the road for 20 days. There must be something he could do.

"Madam," he replied, "there are millions of refugees all over China."

"But these are children!" she cried.

"If you wish to go farther," he said, "the only way is across those mountains." There was only one pass open, he said, and it ran through a battle line, with Japanese troops on one side and Chinese on the other. But he kindly offered to provide Gladys with two soldiers for protection if she chose to attempt the journey.

Gladys looked up. The mountaintops were so high they were hidden by clouds. It would be a steep trek for the children. But there was no other way.

Gladys, the children, and the soldiers made it safely through the pass with only a few minor injuries due to slipping and sliding. After one final, dangerous train ride in some coal cars through Japanese-controlled territory, they arrived safely in Sian.

But the older children were concerned for Gladys. "For days you have been ill," they said. "You have carried one child, sometimes two, all day, and you have given nearly all the food to us."

Gladys ignored their concerns. She also ignored the suggestions of the orphanage workers who urged her to stay and rest. As the children were now in good hands, Gladys thought her job was to continue traveling throughout the villages, holding meetings.

She left the orphanage, found a village . . . and woke up in a hospital. She had collapsed while preaching. The doctor told her she should have died long before: she was suffering from a combination of fever, exhaustion, malnutrition, typhus, and pneumonia.

It took Gladys many years to fully recover. Yet she continued to speak publicly and help Chinese refugees throughout the war, as well as prisoners and lepers.

As the world war came to a close, a civil war began in China, fought between the Chinese Communists and the Chinese Nationalists. On October 1, 1949, Communist leader Mao Zedong declared victory, while Nationalist leader Chiang Kai-shek and his troops retreated to the island of Taiwan.

One day, shortly after the Communist takeover, Gladys witnessed the authorities behead 200 college students, some of them her friends, who were recent Christian converts. Because of their new faith, they had refused to swear loyalty to the Communist Party.

When Communist authorities began to zero in on Gladys as well, she left for Great Britain. There she did all she could to help Chinese refugees: she rescued a wrongly imprisoned Chinese woman in Belfast and opened a Chinese church in London. She also held meetings where she requested clothing donations for those who had fled mainland China and were now crowded into refugee camps in Formosa, Hong Kong, and Taiwan.

After 10 years in the West, she tried to return to mainland China but was refused entry. So instead she worked in an orphanage in Taiwan.

In 1957, a writer named Alan Burgess published a biography about Gladys that was made into a film starring Ingrid Bergman. Gladys was mortified by the fictional elements of the film, which portrayed her friendship with Linnan as a romance.

Gladys wrote her memoir in 1970, the same year she died in Taiwan, at the age of 68.

LEARN MORE

─────────── ★ ───────────

Gladys Aylward: The Adventure of a Lifetime by Janet and Geoff Benge (YWAM, 1998).

The Little Woman by Gladys Aylward, with Christine Hunter (Moody, 1970).

The Small Woman: The Heroic Story of Gladys Aylward by Alan Burgess (Reprint Society, 1957).

"Yangcheng and the Inn of the Eight Happinesses," CJVlang, https://archive.is/vcX6l. Includes photos taken in 2006 of the inn's remains.

PART II

The United States and the Philippines

ELIZABETH MacDONALD

Pearl Harbor Reporter and OSS Agent

REPORTER ELIZABETH MacDonald, on assignment in Honolulu, was in bed on the morning of Sunday, December 7, 1941, listening to a radio broadcast of the Mormon Tabernacle Choir. Suddenly an announcer cut in. "The islands are under attack," he said. "This is the real McCoy." Elizabeth didn't think it was the real *anything*; she was sure it was just another army maneuver. But a few minutes later, she received a call from her photographer at Scripps Howard News Service. He wasn't sure which country was doing the bombing, Germany or Japan, but he did know that the US naval base at Pearl Harbor was under attack.

During the first half of their drive to Pearl Harbor, Elizabeth and the photographer didn't notice anything unusual; it was a typically quiet Sunday morning.

But when they got closer, Elizabeth saw something shocking. Reporting later, she described it as "a formation of black planes diving straight into the ocean off Pearl Harbor. The blue sky was punctured with anti-aircraft smoke puffs." It was the second wave of Japanese bombers. Looking over her shoulder, Elizabeth suddenly saw "a rooftop fly into the air."

Elizabeth MacDonald interviews a US sailor in Honolulu. *Elizabeth MacDonald McIntosh*

She wrote that she now understood "that numb terror that all of London has known for months. It is the terror of not being able to do anything but fall on your stomach and hope the bomb won't land on you."

"Bombs were still dropping over the city," Elizabeth wrote, "as ambulances screamed off into the heart of the destruction. The drivers were blood-sodden when they returned, with stories of streets ripped up, houses burned, twisted shrapnel and charred bodies of children."

The Japanese had targeted the battleships in Pearl Harbor and the nearby airfields, not civilians. But because the Japanese

★★★

TOJO'S SPEECH

As President Franklin Roosevelt's famous "Date of Infamy" speech, given the day after Pearl Harbor, was meant to form public opinion and give national direction for the war, so was the speech of Japanese prime minister Hideki Tojo, broadcast in Japanese cinemas on the evening of the attacks. In his speech he claimed that despite Japan's best efforts, "the peace of the whole of East Asia has collapsed." He went on to blame Japan's new military aggression in the Far East on the US demands that Japan withdraw from China and annul their Tripartite Pact with Germany and Italy. "Should the [Japanese] Empire give in to all [US] demands" he said, "not only would Japan lose its prestige and fail to see the China Incident [Japan's undeclared war with China] to its completion, but its very existence would be in peril."

★★★

destroyed most of the US planes before they could get airborne and do battle, frantic US military personnel on the ground tried to shoot the Japanese down with anti-aircraft guns. Some of their misfired ammunition destroyed buildings, killed 68 civilians, and wounded 35.

Elizabeth was not allowed near Pearl Harbor—the US military did not want female journalists on the front lines of military action—so she focused instead on the civilian casualties in the area and the desperate attempts to save them.

"The blood-soaked drivers returned with stories of streets ripped up, houses burned, twisted shrapnel and charred bodies

★★★

PEARL HARBOR'S IMPACT ON AMERICAN ISOLATIONISM

The Japanese knew they could never defeat America in a long war, but they bombed Pearl Harbor hoping the destruction would prevent the US Navy from immediately interfering in their intended domination of the Far East. The US Navy was indeed badly damaged, but because this surprise military strike—widely referred to at the time as a "sneak attack"—occurred before a formal declaration of war and because it caused the death of approximately 2,500 Americans, it united the nation behind the war effort as little else could have. Before Pearl Harbor, many Americans were isolationist, set against entering World War II to help Britain defend itself from Nazi Germany. After Pearl Harbor, American isolationism virtually disappeared.

★★★

of children," she wrote. In the morgue, Elizabeth saw bodies "laid on slabs in the grotesque positions in which they had died. Fear contorted their faces."

As Elizabeth watched firefighters bring victims inside—some of them with the acronym DOA (dead on arrival) marked on their foreheads—she wrote that life had suddenly become "blood and the fear of death—and death itself. . . . In the emergency room . . . doctors calmly continued to treat the victims of this new war. Interns were taping up windows to prevent them from crashing into the emergency area as bombs fell and the dead and wounded continued to arrive."

When Elizabeth left the emergency room and returned to Honolulu, she saw that many familiar shops had burned down. After dusk, she described "the all-night horror of attack in the dark. Sirens shrieking, sharp, crackling police reports and the tension of a city wrapped in fear."

No one knew if the attack on Pearl Harbor was the first part of a bigger Japanese invasion plan. Hawaii was far from the US mainland and could have easily been overrun by the Japanese. "In the nightmare of Monday and Tuesday," Elizabeth wrote, "there was the struggle to keep normal when planes zoomed overhead and guns cracked out at an unseen enemy. There was blackout and suspicion riding the back of wild rumors: Parachutists in the hills! Poison in your food!"

In order to help prevent a possible invasion, Elizabeth, along with many others, placed barbed wire along Oahu's beaches. Blackouts were ordered every night. Car headlights had to be dimmed, although most people couldn't drive their cars anyway because gasoline was suddenly in short supply. Censorship prevented Elizabeth from sending out any news stories for several weeks.

★★

EXECUTIVE ORDER #9066

The hysteria that followed the Pearl Harbor attack gave rise to unfounded suspicions that Japanese Americans living on the West Coast may have helped guide the attacking Japanese planes and also might offer strategic intelligence to Japan during a potential land invasion. On February 19, 1942, President Roosevelt issued Executive Order

Newspapers announcing the impending relocation of Japanese Americans living on the West Coast. *National Archives*

#9066, which forced West Coast Japanese Americans—more than 100,000 in all—out of their homes (which most were never able to reclaim) and into hastily constructed, barracks-style internment camps in remote areas.

While the government provided them with basic necessities, the lack of privacy, the barbed wire, and the armed guards stationed on the outer perimeter of the camps made these people—more than half of them US citizens—acutely aware they were being imprisoned in their own country and without a trial, a basic right guaranteed by the US Constitution.

Although Japanese Americans were barred from military service immediately following the Pearl Harbor attack, beginning in January 1943, more than 32,000 (most from the camps, some from other areas) volunteered for or were drafted into the US military. The 442nd Regimental Combat Team, composed almost exclusively of Japanese American soldiers, became one of the most highly decorated units in the history of the US Army.

★★★

But the Japanese did not follow the air attack with a ground invasion (although they did invade the Aleutian Islands, a US territory, six months later). And Elizabeth's report was not published: her editors thought that its graphic descriptions would shock readers.

After things had calmed down somewhat, Elizabeth's employer at Scripps Howard News asked her to report to Washington, DC, her hometown. The atmosphere in the US capital was strikingly different from that in Hawaii. No one in Washington was living in fear; the only signs of war were the rations on sugar and gasoline.

While covering an exhibit for the Department of Agriculture, Elizabeth met a military officer, a major. Their conversation turned to Pearl Harbor. When he discovered that Elizabeth had been there during the attack, he asked her opinion of the Japanese who lived in Hawaii: Were they disloyal Americans? "Definitely not," Elizabeth said. She told him she had lived with a Japanese professor and his wife in Honolulu for more than a year while covering the war and that they'd taught her some Japanese.

When he heard this, the major looked at Elizabeth intently and asked her a surprising question: Would she like to make a significant contribution to the war effort? It would be secret government work, he said, so he couldn't go into any immediate details. But he was so certain Elizabeth would qualify, he handed her three applications. "Fill them out immediately," he said, "and mail them to the Office of Strategic Services. Time is of the essence." Then he disappeared.

Elizabeth applied and was accepted. The Office of Strategic Services—or the OSS—was a new espionage organization, ordered into existence by President Roosevelt and headed by General Bill Donovan, a highly decorated veteran of World War I.

On her first day at the OSS offices in Washington, Elizabeth learned from an officer that she would be working in the field of psychological warfare, the OSS's Morale Operations—or MO—division. MO, Elizabeth was told, was "the art of influencing enemy thinking by means of 'black propaganda': presenting misleading information as coming from within the enemy's own ranks." In other words, Elizabeth would create lies: false newspaper clippings supposedly printed in Japan; orders appearing to have come from the Japanese high command; or rumors geared to create disillusionment with the war. Elizabeth learned that measuring the results of her work would be nearly impossible: "Even the best interrogators," she would write later, "could not determine just what made a Japanese surrender: starvation, loss of blood, disease, temporary insanity, or that phony and purely coincidental MO clipping in his pocket."

Elizabeth learned of the significant role psychological warfare had played during the German invasion of Europe in 1940. During the Battle of France, she was told, German agents created rumors of premature German victories and false newspapers declaring the collapse of England.

The OSS was doing similar work in the Far East. An officer explained to Elizabeth that MO was most effective when integrated with military strategy. For instance, if the OSS knew the Allies were going to make a landing in Shanghai, MO would create a series of rumors—sent out in easily deciphered codes—to make the Japanese believe they were really going to land elsewhere.

Elizabeth was encouraged to use her imagination. "Out of twenty wild schemes," the instructing officer said, "there might be one that would really work—and save lives."

The people working in MO were chosen from a wide variety of backgrounds, "rare strange personalities," Elizabeth wrote later, "selected at grab-bag random from all corners of the world." But "together they fitted into the over-all jigsaw picture." Among the people Elizabeth encountered that first day were a Chinese artist, a Thai missionary, a newspaper reporter, a Shanghai businessman, a private detective, a radio show producer, two lawyers, an Olympic broad jumper, and a Japanese American who had fought with General Donovan during World War I.

One day, Elizabeth and two male OSS agents were going through the contents of a sack. It had been in the possession of a starved Japanese battalion recently defeated by the British in Burma. Among the brass dog tags, pictures of children, and good-luck charms, Elizabeth found a leather pouch. Inside was a large batch of postcards. The cards—written in pencil and not containing any significant military messages—had been stamped with a Japanese army post office star and cleared by a censor. Since there were so many, one of the agents thought the men had probably been ordered to write home before their final battle.

Elizabeth said what a shame it was that the postcards couldn't be mailed anyway. Suddenly, an idea hit all three agents at once. "Why *can't* they be mailed to Japan?" Elizabeth elaborated on this idea. "Erase the original messages!" she said. "Substitute our own. It could be the first black MO into Japan!"

They recruited a group of 10 nisei—Americans born to Japanese immigrants—to help them change the messages. Elizabeth told them that the messages should all mention how difficult the war was in Burma, how they were all starving in the jungles, and how they felt unsupported by those back home.

One of the nisei, a man named Saburo, showed Elizabeth a card that bore a message from a soldier to his wife. The soldier had written that he hoped she would tell their son, whom he had never met, that his father was proud to die for the emperor.

"It's so sad—I hate to change it," Saburo said.

Elizabeth couldn't help feeling sad too. But she firmly believed, as she told Saburo, that "whatever heartbreak we might bring to one person would be well worth the effort if we could plant a small doubt back home in the minds of the people that Burma was lost and something was radically wrong with their war effort." These postcards might help shorten the war.

Saburo changed the message to the following: "Don't ever tell our son I died for a lost cause."

Elizabeth was eventually transferred from Washington to India. Six weeks after arriving, she received a new project. She was given an intelligence report regarding the extremely difficult conditions the Japanese troops in Burma were experiencing: poor food, short supplies, and little outside news.

Elizabeth already knew that Tojo Hideki, Japan's prime minister, had resigned. The troops in Burma must have heard this news, but they wouldn't yet have received any related details.

She suddenly got an idea. During Tojo's time as prime minister, any member of the Japanese military who surrendered to the enemy would be executed or banished—part of the reason Japanese soldiers seldom surrendered.

Elizabeth typed up the draft of a forgery that stated the following: penalties for surrender had been lifted with Tojo's resignation. The new prime minister, Koiso Kuniaki, had instituted new regulations, making it allowable for Japanese soldiers to surrender in certain situations.

Now she needed someone to write the order in Japanese. Another agent named Bill introduced Elizabeth to a college-educated Japanese prisoner named Okamoto with whom Bill had once attended school. Okamoto had surrendered in Burma out of disgust with the bungled campaign. He was willing to work with the Allies only because he thought doing so would help end the war quickly, which would in turn save Japanese lives. Okamoto took Elizabeth's draft and after several days of work, produced a perfect forgery on the same type of paper on which all Japanese military business was written.

A Burmese OSS double agent, code-named Roger, who was pretending to work for the Japanese in Burma, assassinated a courier working for the Japanese, and slipped the communication into the dead man's bag. He then alerted Japanese headquarters in Burma of the man's murder. The courier's pouch was brought to the company commander, who opened it and read the forgery. Roger saw him speak rapidly to the other officers in the room.

OSS agents made additional efforts to get the forged document behind Japanese lines in Burma: they copied it and littered the Burmese jungles with it.

Roger later told Elizabeth he was certain the forgery was directly responsible for the altered behavior of the Japanese soldiers in Burma toward the end of the campaign: many of them surrendered without a struggle when clearly outnumbered. POW camps, usually empty, suddenly became overcrowded. "As the Burma campaign closed," Roger told Elizabeth, "reports of fanatical, last-ditch fighting were rare." Many lives on both sides were saved.

A few years after the war, Elizabeth wrote her memoir. In 1998, she wrote a collective biography under her married name, McIntosh, regarding other OSS women. And on December 6, 2012, her Pearl Harbor report was finally published by the *Washington Post*.

Elizabeth lived for many years in the Washington, DC, area, where she continued to write on her vintage typewriter. She died there on June 8, 2015, at the age of 100.

LEARN MORE

"Honolulu After Pearl Harbor: A Report Published for the First Time, 71 Years Later" by Elizabeth McIntosh, *Washington Post*, December 6, 2012, www.washingtonpost.com/opinions/honolulu-after-pearl-harbor-a-report-published-for-the-first-time-71-years-later/2012/12/06/e9029986-3d69-11e2-bca3-aadc9b7e29c5_story.html.

OSS Undercover Girl: Elizabeth P. McIntosh, an Interview by Bob Bergin (Banana Tree, 2012), Kindle e-book.

Sisterhood of Spies by Elizabeth McIntosh (Naval Institute Press, 1998).

Undercover Girl by Elizabeth MacDonald (Macmillan, 1947).

DENNY WILLIAMS

American Nurse Under Fire

IT WAS THE MORNING of May 6, 1942. In a few hours, the US Army stationed on the Philippine island of Corregidor would surrender to the army of Imperial Japan.

But the fighting men would not be the only ones involved in this surrender. Along with them were female nurses, some of them civilians but most of them official members of the US Army. None of these women had been trained in combat nursing and yet they had endured months of just that. Now they awaited their fate. They were all too aware of the horrors the Japanese army inflicted on Chinese women four and a half years earlier during the Nanking Massacre. Tomorrow they would be facing the same enemy. Were they now living their last hours? If so, would anyone ever know what they had endured during the past grueling months?

They wanted to leave proof that they had been alive before meeting the Japanese face-to-face. One of them tore a large square from a bedsheet. Another wrote the following words at the top: "Members of the Army Nurse Corps and Civilian women who were in the Malinta Tunnel when Corregidor fell." Then 69 women signed their names. One of them was Denny Williams.

On December 8, 1941, Denny, a former US Army nurse trained to administer anesthesia during surgeries, was living in Manila with her husband Bill. That morning she received two phone calls that would change the course of her life. The first was from her husband's boss at Caltex Oil, where Bill worked as an executive. The Japanese had just bombed Pearl Harbor. The second call was from the chief nurse of Sternberg, the US Army hospital in Manila. Was Denny willing to help them if the Philippine islands also came under attack?

A portion of the bedsheet signed by the nurses at Corregidor on May 6, 1942. Denny Williams's name is in the middle of the third column.
AMEDD Center of History and Heritage, Archival Repository

She was. And a few hours later Denny encountered her first war victims at Sternberg. They were young American men who had been attempting to defend Clark Field, the US Air Force base placed in the Philippines to protect the Far East from Japanese aggression. The Japanese destroyed it in less than an hour.

Bill, a reserve first lieutenant with the 31st infantry, joined his unit. He asked Denny to leave for the safety of the United States. She refused.

After Manila was declared an "open city"—that is, all fighting would stop and the city saved from destruction—American and Filipino servicemen, including Bill, left the city via trucks, buses, and boats. They headed for the Bataan Peninsula and the nearby fortress on Corregidor Island to continue the fight.

Sternberg, because it was an army hospital, also evacuated much of its staff and patients to Bataan and Corregidor.

Denny followed and began working at the US Army hospital on Bataan known as No. 2. It was like no other hospital that Denny had ever seen or worked in: it was outdoors, in an area of dense jungle beside a river. The only way to access it was via a crude carabao (water buffalo) trail, and each of the wards was labeled with a number hammered onto a banyan tree. The nurses were often visited by small animals during the night and were attacked by insects all through the day.

Generators and other equipment had been brought from Manila during the evacuation. Everything else—tables, desks, beds, chairs—was soon crafted out of bamboo by local civilian Filipino craftsmen.

After the evacuation to Bataan, all army personnel had their rations cut in half. This was going to be a long fight, many Filipino civilians had followed the army, and supplies needed to last as long as possible.

The amount of work performed by the hungry medical staff seemed endless. At No. 2, surgeries were performed round the clock for wounded fighting men: six surgeons did as many as 420 operations during a 24-hour period. And Denny was there to administer the necessary anesthetics. But if there was ever a surgical lull, she would attend patients in the jungle wards. At this point most of them were recovering from shrapnel wounds or suffering from a combination of diseases related to their environment and malnutrition: malaria, dysentery, and beriberi.

No. 2 was located near two US airfields that were often targeted by Japanese bombers. Once, while Denny was bathing alone in the river, she was nearly gunned down by a low-flying Japanese plane. As she scrambled for the nearest bush, narrowly avoiding the falling branch of a hit tree, she realized, for the first time, how desperate their situation really was.

The Japanese were determined that all the American and Filipino defenders should understand this. One morning, after the area around No. 2 had suffered some intensive bombing, Denny and the other hospital personnel found copies of a leaflet strewn on the ground, officially addressed to General Douglas MacArthur, head of the US forces on Bataan and Corregidor, but obviously meant for all the Americans and Filipinos in the area.

"You are well aware that you are doomed," it read, "the question is how long you will be able to resist. You have already cut rations in half. . . . Your presence and honor have been upheld. However, in order to avoid needless bloodshed and save your . . . troops, you are advised to surrender."

Denny was exhausted and racked with headaches, not only from being on her feet 20 hours a day but also from gnawing hunger. All the nurses were slightly gaunt. But "until the bayonet was at our throats," Denny wrote later, "we wouldn't give up."

Instead of surrendering, the forces on Bataan mounted a fierce defense, pounding the Japanese invaders with a barrage of artillery fire.

On January 15, the Bataan defenders received a message from General MacArthur, who was in his headquarters in the Malinta Tunnel on Corregidor:

> Help is on the way from the United States. Thousands of troops and hundreds of planes are being dispatched. The exact time of arrival of reinforcement is unknown as they will have to fight their way through Japanese attempts against them. It is imperative that our troops hold until these reinforcements arrive. . . .
>
> It is a question now of courage and of determination. Men who . . . fight will save themselves and their country.
>
> I call upon every soldier in Bataan to fight in his assigned position, resisting every attack. . . . If we will fight we will win; if we retreat we will be destroyed.

This message was greeted with cheering, hugs, and applause. Victory was certain!

But after time passed and no help arrived, it was difficult to continue to believe MacArthur's promise. And during a rare visit with her husband, Denny realized that the Bataan defenders had stopped believing it long before. Bill recited a grim poem that had become popular among the Bataan defenders:

> *We're the battling bastards of Bataan;*
> *No momma, no poppa, no Uncle Sam;*
> *No aunts, no uncles, no nephews, no nieces;*
> *No rifles, no guns or artillery pieces.*
> *And nobody gives a damn.*

★★

THE ARCADIA CONFERENCE AND
THE HEROES OF BATAAN

Japan's surprise attack on Pearl Harbor created a shocked sense of helplessness in a nation not used to losing battles. The press quickly diverted America's attention to the Bataan defenders, heroically struggling against impossible odds. But while these men were fighting for their lives, plans were being made in Washington to abandon them. During the Arcadia Conference—December 22, 1941, through January 14, 1942—US and British leaders decided on the "Europe first" strategy; that is, the war against Nazi Germany would be given priority over the war against Imperial Japan. But in order to keep American home-front morale up, to protect Australia from invasion, and to encourage US allies in the Far East, the Americans on Bataan were fed lies and never directly told of this decision. Writing about them in his diary, US secretary of war Henry Stimson stated, "There are times when men have to die."

★★

Although Denny gently chided Bill for his lack of faith, shortly afterward she realized the poem's painful truth. While listening to President Franklin Roosevelt on the radio in February, they heard him imply that the US military was going to send troops, ships, and supplies to aid the European war instead of to the one raging on Bataan.

Denny and the other nurses finally accepted this cold, hard fact: "We were expendable."

But neither the men nor their nurses gave up, even when, on March 14, they heard more discouraging news: MacArthur had left Bataan on a PT (patrol torpedo) boat on March 11 for the safety of Australia.

A few days later, the Japanese again urged the Bataan defenders to surrender. They littered Bataan with cans, each one containing a letter from Japanese General Homma Masaharu addressed to the new commander of the Allied forces in the Philippines, General Jonathan Wainwright:

> We have the honor to address you in accordance with Bushido—the code of the Japanese warrior. . . . You have already fought to the best of your ability. . . . Accept our sincere advice and save the lives of those officers and men

★★

"I CAME THROUGH AND I SHALL RETURN"

General MacArthur was so determined to stay with his men to the last that President Roosevelt, concerned at what might happen to this famous general in Japanese hands, finally issued him a direct evacuation order. After arriving in Australia, MacArthur gave a speech in which he implied Roosevelt was planning to send him back in a more effective manner. The words with which he ended the speech— "I came through and I shall return"—greatly irritated the president, who had no specific plans of allowing MacArthur to do so. But these words were embraced by many Filipinos throughout the occupation.

★★

under your command. . . . If a reply to this advisory note is not received . . . by noon March 22, 1942 we shall consider ourselves at liberty to take any action whatsoever.

"Most of us," Denny wrote, "expected to be taken prisoner right where we were. After that, we didn't care to contemplate. . . . And yet nobody really gave up."

Describing the next few weeks, Denny wrote, "The battle was now so close we could hear the detonations and feel concussions from the big artillery. Bombs dropped every few minutes and we grew used to the whistle of flying steel." They were now "so tired and starved [they] walked like zombies." The tattered US and Filipino casualties now coming into No. 2 had a haunted look in their eyes. They had seen the enemy up close. They had heard their fierce battle cry: "Banzai! Banzai!" ["One thousand years! One thousand years!"—many years to the emperor and his reign].

On the evening of April 8, Denny and the other Bataan nurses received orders from General Wainwright to evacuate to the island of Corregidor. The American and Filipino men fighting on the Bataan Peninsula, under the direct command of General Edward King, were planning to surrender to the Japanese.

Denny first had a visit to pay. Bill had recently arrived at No. 2 with a bad case of malaria.

"We're leaving," Denny whispered to Bill. "It's supposed to be a secret from the patients. Bill, I don't want to go." It wasn't just leaving Bill that bothered her. There were thousands of men still recovering at No. 2. What would these sick men do without anyone to care for them? Some nurses seriously considered disobeying General Wainwright's orders. They felt it directly contradicted the pledge they had taken when first becoming nurses to never leave their patients.

"Of course you're going," Bill said. "This means surrender. It's inevitable."

They parted sadly. Then Denny and the other nurses from Bataan hospitals No. 1 and No. 2 made their way to the fortress on Corregidor Island.

At this point there were 12,000 people—fighting men, civilians, and medical personnel—crowded into the individual tunnels or "laterals" of the Malinta Tunnel on Corregidor. The Bataan nurses initially felt a sense of safety there: not only did they finally have a ceiling and walls, but the fortress was carved out of rock.

But now that Bataan was defeated, the Japanese focused all their attention—and bombers—on Corregidor. The Malinta Tunnel was bombed unceasingly. Flakes of shattered concrete and dust particles filled the air, making it difficult to breathe. The nurses developed headaches from the thunderous noise

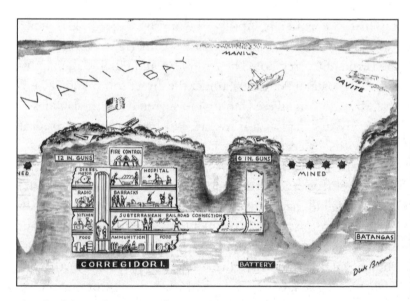

Sketch of the Malinta Tunnel. *National Archives*

and fever blisters from a combination of perspiration, filth, and malnutrition.

Yet, as the Corregidor defenders soldiered on, so did the nurses who, for long, weary hours sorted patients, gave injections, assisted operations, only to watch many patients die from shock. Denny continued to function only "by blocking out all emotion."

She occasionally saw General Wainwright walking through the tunnels. She noticed his sad expression whenever he passed a severely wounded soldier.

The nurses were drilled in putting on their gas masks in case the Japanese lobbed poison gas into the tunnel. Denny was "petrified." Yet she noticed that "no nurse voiced her fears."

Then the inevitable happened. On May 6, 1942, the nurses were told that official surrender would take place at noon. "Compared to Bataan a month ago," Denny wrote, "this was devastatingly final. Then we'd had a place to flee to, now we had nowhere. . . . I thought of brutality, pain, and rape, of naked bayonets and poison gas."

Just before the surrender, Denny went to the main tunnel. The men—gaunt, disheveled, and dirty—were about to give themselves up to an enemy of rumored cruelty. They asked the nurses for food and water. There was now little of either.

Then, finally, the enemy arrived. The Japanese officers had swords hanging from their waists. The Japanese soldiers carried guns with bayonets. They ordered the nurses to turn around and face the wall.

But to Denny's surprise and relief, aside from one failed midnight assault, the women were not harmed. Only one aspect of these women seemed to fascinate the Japanese: they were in uniform. The nurses had obviously endured the strain of war along with the men. To discover how they had managed, each of them was interviewed extensively.

The only serious demand made of them was a low bow from the waist whenever they found themselves in the presence of any Japanese. Soldiers patrolled the tunnel constantly, often coming into proximity with the nurses to ensure that this order was carried out.

Eventually, though, Denny came to realize "the Japanese were only men like other men, some good, some bad; and that the brutality of war brought out the brutality—if it was there— in any man."

The nurses continued working in the Malinta Tunnel till the end of June, discharging their patients one by one into the hands of the enemy. Then they moved the remaining patients to a bombed-out shell of an old hospital nearby called Fort Mills.

They still hoped their military would rescue them. When Denny fell sick at Fort Mills, she asked her doctor in a whisper when he thought this might happen.

He looked at her strangely. "Denny, Denny, are you delirious?" he asked. "It'll be a long time before we get out of this, months, maybe years." Then he lowered his voice, "Don't you know we're losing this bloody war? . . . In time, we'll win, of course. But for now we're cut off."

Denny hoped he was wrong. But the following years proved the young doctor's words to be painfully accurate. On July 2, 1942, the nurses were imprisoned in the Santo Tomas internment camp in Manila, where they tried, as much as possible, to help the other prisoners as they all struggled to survive on starvation rations.

Finally, on the evening of February 3, 1945, US troops liberated Santo Tomas. They came too late for many of the prisoners, who had by then died of ailments related to undernourishment. All of the Bataan-Corregidor nurses survived.

Some of the nurses on their way out of Santo Tomas internment camp, wearing newly issued uniforms. *AMEDD Center of History and Heritage, Archival Repository*

On Sunday, February 11, 1945, American lieutenant colonel Nola Forrest told the gaunt, exhausted, but elated nurses to be ready for departure on the following morning. She also mentioned that US intelligence officials, who realized these women had never been trained for combat nursing, were eager to debrief them. "You're the first [US military] women to have served under actual combat conditions," she said. "Whatever tips you have on how you survived could be of great help to others."

All the nurses would be promoted to a higher military rank, Forrest said, and would receive the Presidential Citation and a Bronze Star.

After the war, Denny discovered that Bill had been killed with other American POWs while aboard one of Japan's cruel "Hell ships." The unmarked ship had been targeted and sunk by an American bomber.

Denny found solace by returning to the military. She worked for US Army hospitals stateside and overseas until the early 1960s, when she retired with the rank of lieutenant colonel. She died in Texas in 1997.

LEARN MORE

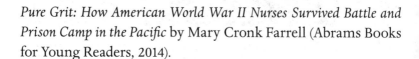

Pure Grit: How American World War II Nurses Survived Battle and Prison Camp in the Pacific by Mary Cronk Farrell (Abrams Books for Young Readers, 2014).

To the Angels by Denny Williams (Denson Press, 1985).

We Band of Angels: The Untold Story of American Nurses Trapped on Bataan by the Japanese by Elizabeth M. Norman (Pocket Books, 1999).

MARGARET UTINSKY

The Miss U Network

MARGARET UTINSKY PEERED out the window of her second-floor apartment. On the street below, Japanese officers questioned everyone who passed by. They were rounding up "enemy aliens": British and American citizens. Margaret had no intention of being among them. She could afford to wait a long time; her apartment was stocked with food and medical supplies provided by personnel working at the US military bases in Manila who had been anxious to prevent their supplies from assisting the invading enemy.

Margaret, a Red Cross nurse by day and the operator of a servicemen's canteen by night, had taken taxi-loads of those supplies, hoping to open her canteen again when the fighting was over. She wanted to be of help, especially to her husband, Jack, a civil engineer with the US military in Manila who had urged Margaret to evacuate with the other military wives when the

Margaret Utinsky.
Miss U by Margaret Utinsky (Naylor, 1948)

Japanese first attacked. Margaret had refused. Later, when Manila was declared an open city and Jack was ordered to pull back to the Bataan Peninsula with the rest of the military, Margaret refused his urgent suggestion to stay at the local hotel with the other American and British civilians; she assumed—correctly—that the Japanese would round them up and force them into an internment camp. And Margaret didn't see how she could be of any use to Jack in an internment camp.

After the Japanese searched through the first floor of the apartment building and found all the apartments vacated, they didn't bother checking the second floor. So Margaret remained hidden there for 10 weeks, watching and waiting in near silence while quietly listening to the official radio station of the USAFFE (the United States Army Forces in the Far East), called The Voice of Freedom, airing from the Malinta Tunnel on the island of Corregidor. The broadcasts were at first upbeat and confident:

the United States would certainly send help to rescue the out-numbered American and Filipino men fighting on Bataan.

But as time went on and no help came, the optimism of the broadcasts sounded forced and empty. One day in May, Margaret heard the last transmission: "The men of Corregidor have fought a gallant fight. . . . They fought on and on, expecting the help which never came. Now they must surrender, leaving their dead."

Margaret was determined to find Jack. But she first needed a new identity that would enable her to avoid arrest. Since the name Utinsky was Lithuanian, Margaret decided to become Rosena Utinsky, a citizen of Lithuania who couldn't speak the language because she had been orphaned and raised by a Canadian aunt.

Then she joined a small team of Red Cross Filipino doctors and nurses traveling to war-torn Bataan in order to create emergency clinics for Filipino civilians desperately in need of medical attention. The war had caused shortages of food and medicine, and Bataan was now raging with epidemics of malaria and dysentery.

The Bataan civilians who visited the clinic had a shocking tale: after the surrender of the Americans and Filipinos at Bataan, Japanese soldiers had forced the emaciated soldiers along the road. If Filipino civilians, watching by the side of the road, were caught offering them food or water, they were killed. Many prisoners collapsed. When they did, the Japanese soldiers would bayonet or shoot them or leave them where they were to be run over by oncoming trucks. Sometimes the Japanese would deliberately stop the march in front of a natural water spring by the side of the road and then shoot any desperately thirsty man who tried to steal a drink. One witness told Margaret they'd

★★★

THE BATAAN DEATH MARCH

The most infamous war crime to befall US servicemen during World War II wasn't preplanned. The Japanese had estimated transportation needs for approximately 25,000 prisoners. When they were faced with more than 70,000, the prisoners were marched instead. Approximately 60,000 Filipinos and 10,000 Americans, who had together defended Bataan on half rations for four months, were now forced to walk 65 miles in the hot sun with little food, water, or rest. The increasing cruelty exhibited by the Japanese guards toward the exhausted men along the way was the result of (1) the brutality they had each experienced during their military training and (2) their deep lack of respect for anyone who chose surrender over death. Approximately 700 Americans and 10,000 Filipinos died during what the survivors would always grimly refer to as "the hike." Sixteen thousand more desperately weakened Filipinos and Americans would die during their first week at their destination, Camp O'Donnell.

★★★

seen a group of men being pushed into a latrine; their comrades had been forced to bury them alive.

As Margaret worked with the Red Cross team, she became obsessed with a single thought: "I knew that I could not stop," she wrote later, "until I had given every ounce of my strength to help the men who still lived. After what [they] had endured, nothing seemed too hard or too dangerous." And she felt certain that Jack was among the survivors.

On a second Red Cross trip to the area, Margaret applied for the position of field nurse, someone who would visit local civilians in their homes. Traveling from place to place would enable her, she hoped, to gain information about the American prisoners.

She discovered that the Japanese granted the prisoners one privilege: every few days they were allowed to leave the camp and forage for themselves. The guards didn't think they would try to escape: they were too starved to get very far.

One day, on her way to one of the Red Cross tents, Margaret met two gaunt American officers. She fed them and quietly filled their pockets with drugs and food from the Red Cross's supplies. She had to be careful: the Japanese did not allow the Filipino Red Cross to help Americans.

Then she asked them to provide her with two lists: the names of American prisoners who had died in the death march and those who still lived. A few days later, three US soldiers came to the clinic and handed Margaret the lists. Jack's name wasn't on either one. They didn't know where he was. They also told her that they were being sent to a place called Camp O'Donnell, where the death march survivors were imprisoned.

Margaret kept in contact with the men and finally learned that Jack had been in the Bilibid prison in Manila for a few days. No one knew where he was now. But he was alive, Margaret was sure of that.

How could she help him? Margaret received her answer to that question in the form of a letter from a Filipino Red Cross doctor, Dr. Romeo Y. Atienza, with whom she had worked during one of her relief expeditions on Bataan. The Japanese were allowing him to visit the Filipino prisoners inside Camp O'Donnell. While forbidden to help the Americans, he did observe them. They were clearly starving to death. The Japanese were making a show of allowing them to survive: they paid them a small amount of money in exchange for working in the prison garden, tending crops that provided food only for the Japanese guards. However, the wages couldn't purchase nearly enough food to keep the prisoners healthy. And if the starving men didn't work, they received no pay.

Dr. Atenzia had an idea. The Japanese, in a show of racial unity, were releasing Filipino soldiers, who had fought with the Americans, in stages from Camp O'Donnell. Filipino men too weak to leave on foot were transported out in a truck or ambulance. The vehicles were always searched carefully on their way out—but never on the way back in. If Margaret could get supplies to Dr. Atenzia, he could smuggle them into the camp inside the returning ambulances and secretly distribute them to the Americans.

Margaret took the supplies stashed in her Manila apartment, loaded them into bags, bundles, and a trunk, and transported them via multiple train rides. She told curious fellow travelers each time that they were for newly released Filipino prisoners.

At Dr. Atienza's suggestion, Margaret sent a note in with the first "shipment" of supplies, requesting a receipt to make sure the Americans received them. She signed the note "Miss U." The same day, she received a receipt. The men had received the supplies! And those involved in smuggling these supplies to the Americans in the camp—a number that was constantly growing—were given a new name: the Miss U Network.

Margaret wondered if Jack was receiving any of these supplies. She hadn't heard anything from or about him yet. But she was willing to do anything just in case her actions might be helping him. "Risks did not seem too dangerous," she wrote later, "when I thought of him inside those fences."

In December, Margaret heard that the surviving men were being moved to a new prison complex, consisting of three camps, located near Cabanatuan City. By way of two Filipino contacts in the Miss U Network, Margaret started communicating with an American officer in the prison named Colonel Mack. She sent him a note, asking if he knew anything about the fate of a Jack Utinsky. A note came back:

Dear Miss U:

You have many friends in this place. . . . I am deeply sorry that I have to tell you what I found out. Your husband died here on August 6, 1942. He is buried here in the prison graveyard. . . .

You will be told that he died of tuberculosis. That is not true. The men say that he actually died of starvation. A little more food and medicine, which they would not give him here, might have saved him.

This is terrible news for you, who have, with your unselfish work, been able to save so many others. All of us will always owe you a debt that we can never pay for what you have done.

I do want to say to you that this place is far more dangerous for your work than Camp O'Donnell was. Do not take risks that you took there. If you never do another thing you already have done more than any living person to help our men. My sympathy goes out to you in your grief. God bless you in all you do.

Sincerely yours, Edward Mack,
Lt. Colonel, U.S. Army

Jack had starved to death. Margaret blamed herself. "If he could have received just a little of the food I had given to others," she wrote later, "he might be alive. If I had found him four months sooner, he might be alive."

She became overwhelmed with grief. While she remained involved in the Miss U Network, its leadership gradually shifted to others: Claire Phillips, an American resister (chapter 8), and Ramon Amusategui, a Spanish businessman. Their operation ran smoothly, in part because there were so many resisters involved. But the sheer numbers were what made the work so dangerous for all of them.

Margaret knew she would soon come under suspicion; it was only a matter of time. One day she was visited by someone claiming to be a Filipino guerrilla who needed her help. He showed her the latest edition of an American magazine as proof he was working with the Americans. Then he promised to provide her with money to help the guerrillas. The man's odd presentation and Margaret's sharp intuition made her realize this was a trap.

She told him she didn't need any money.

After he was gone, she found a gun under her typewriter. The visitor must have placed it there. She quickly disposed of it. But she knew what was coming next.

Her phone rang at midnight. When she answered it, the caller hung up. Someone was checking to see if she was still there. Then, at 4:00 AM, 50 Japanese soldiers and officers pounded on the door of her apartment, demanding entry. One of them walked directly to the typewriter and looked under it.

"Where is your gun?" he asked, clearly surprised.

While her apartment was ransacked, Margaret was questioned for hours. Her interrogator was especially interested in her many trips to the prison camps. Before they finally left, they ordered Margaret to stay in Manila. This wasn't over.

A short time later, Margaret was visiting Claire Phillips, who had been hospitalized for a serious infection. Suddenly, a nurse shouted from the hallway, pointing to Margaret, "There are four Japanese soldiers asking for you!" Claire grabbed some incriminating letters from Margaret and stuffed them into her bandages before the soldiers barged in and searched the room. They pointed their bayonets at Margaret. "You will come," they demanded.

She was brought to Fort Santiago, where she was interrogated and tortured for two weeks, before being released and ordered to stay in Manila.

Afraid she might talk if interrogated a second time, Margaret left Manila as soon as possible, fleeing to the mountains to join the guerrillas. As they moved from place to place, always one step ahead of the Japanese, Margaret nursed them as best she could with the supplies at her disposal.

When the American military finally returned to the Philippines, Margaret handed them the POW lists she had collected. These lists helped the military account for the many Americans who had died while imprisoned by the Japanese.

In 1946, Margaret was awarded the Medal of Freedom. She wrote her memoirs in 1948. She died in California in 1970 at the age of 70.

LEARN MORE

Angels of the Underground: The American Women who Resisted the Japanese in the Philippines in World War II by Theresa Kaminski (New York: Oxford, 2016).

Miss U: Angel of the Underground by Margaret Utinsky (Naylor, 1948; e-book, Uncommon Valor, 2014).

POW Angel on Call: The True Story of an American Guerrilla Nurse in the Philippines During WWII by Nancy Polette. A young adult version of *Miss U* (Blessinks, 2013).

YAY PANLILIO

Guerrilla Writer

ONE DAY IN EARLY March 1942, two months into the Japanese occupation of Manila, several Japanese officials walked into the radio station KZRH, also known as Radio Manila. They handed a letter to one of the station's broadcasters, a woman. The letter was addressed to someone named Carlos P. Romulo, a Filipino journalist and the editor and publisher of the *Philippines Herald* who had accurately predicted the Japanese attack on Pearl Harbor and was now US general Douglas MacArthur's press officer. As the "voice" behind the Voice of Freedom radio broadcasts from the Malinta Tunnel on Corregidor Island, Romulo regularly debunked Japanese propaganda and successfully encouraged Filipino resistance. The Japanese had put a price on his head.

The woman at KZRH, a reporter and photographer as well as a broadcaster, had worked for Romulo at the *Philippines Herald*. Did she know where he was now?

She told the Japanese officials she didn't. But she seemed eager to help. If they knew where General MacArthur was, she said, perhaps they would find Romulo nearby. Were they willing to send her to Bataan with a map in order to search for him?

They weren't. They walked out of the station.

The woman was in serious trouble and she knew it. She had been working as an undercover agent for US Army intelligence since before the Japanese invasion of the Philippines. During the first weeks of the Japanese occupation, she broadcast carefully worded messages directed to the Filipino American forces on Bataan, including Romulo, regarding events in occupied Manila. The Japanese high command in Manila hired English-speaking intelligence men in order to understand what they suspected were the woman's coded messages. It was now obvious they had understood too much. She would have to disappear. But there was time for one more broadcast, one more message.

The studio was nearly empty. This final message was for Romulo. She spoke his full name on the air for the first time. She urged him to continue with his resistance work, promising that she would do the same. "We to whom you were a father," she said, "we will keep the faith."

Then she switched off the mike, handed the studio over to the next announcer, and tried not to walk too quickly out of the station. Within 15 minutes, there was an order out for the arrest of Yay Panlilio, journalist, broadcaster, daughter of an American father and Filipino mother, and now the declared enemy of the Empire of Japan.

When the Japanese couldn't locate Yay, they put a price on her head. She hid with an old friend in Manila for four days, then left the city in a blouse and skirt; since she rarely wore women's clothing, it was an excellent disguise. Then she climbed into the mountains. There was nowhere else to go.

The mountains, she knew, were filled with bands of Filipino guerrilla fighters. She would have liked to join them but quickly dismissed the idea. They were constantly on the run from the Japanese, and she knew she wouldn't be able to keep up with them: the year before, while covering a story, she had broken her leg in a serious auto accident, and her bone had not been set properly. She also had a heart condition.

Plus she was a woman. How could she live among hundreds, perhaps thousands, of men?

One night in July 1942, while recovering from malaria on the property of a kind farmer, Yay suddenly encountered a large group of fighters sleeping on the farmer's property. They were so young, they filled her heart with compassion.

Yet, in the morning, she told them to leave for the safety of the farmer and his family. None of them moved. Yay didn't yet realize they were hearing the same thing from everyone: leave for our safety. They told Yay they would make no decision without direct orders from someone they referred to as "the major."

A short time later, Yay met him. He was Marcos Villa Agustin, known as Marking, a former boxer and bus driver who, when the Japanese first attacked, had worked for the Philippine army, convoying troops to Bataan. After his convoy was cut off, he became a scout for the army. When the Japanese captured him and found an American flag and eagle tattooed across his chest, they arrested him. But he managed to escape into the jungle, where other Filipinos eventually gathered to him, forming a guerrilla band.

Marking and Yay connected immediately. He asked her to join his unit. He understood her physical limitations but was determined to assist her with these as best he could, because he knew that her intelligence—and her typewriter—could be

Yay Panlilio and Marking. The Crucible *by Yay Panlilio, Nehalem Valley Historical Society*

powerful weapons. They became a couple. Yay wrote later
about their relationship in this way: "War was our marriage,
the guerillas our sons."

Her years as a Manila-based journalist had given Yay multiple connections; she knew exactly who was loyal to the Filipino
cause and who she could rely on to help. Now she typed dozens
of letters. She asked the wealthy for medicine, food, and money.
To those who excelled at observation she requested information
regarding the Japanese occupation of Manila. She didn't iden-
tify herself openly but provided enough information so that
each recipient would know exactly who had sent it and how to
get back in touch with her. The letters were then delivered by
couriers.

Marking's guerrilla unit was courageous but disorganized.
Yay did what she could to help bring order to the unit, crafting
a "creed" that set official policy:

We, "Marking's Guerrillas," believe it is the right of every
Filipino to walk in dignity, unslapped, unsearched, untied;
to speak freely of honor and injustice alike; to mold our
destiny as a people.

We believe that we owe allegiance to America, and
that the only flags to fly in this sweet air are the Stars and
Stripes and the Philippine flag until such time as the Philippine flag flies alone. . . .

We believe that it is the right of every Filipino to raise
his or her weapon against the enemy, be that weapon
a rifle, a bolo, poison, or a sweet I-don't-know-a-thing
smile. . . .

We believe that the nature and function of the guerrilla is [to] harass the enemy, occupying as many enemy

FILIPINO GUERRILLAS AND THE BATAAN DEATH MARCH

One Filipino guerrilla who witnessed the Bataan Death March claimed it was directly responsible for the formation of Filipino guerrilla units:

> After the march of death was seen by the Bataan people in tears, the people met together to form some sort of association to continue the fight. . . . In the [minds] of a simple people was etched a determination to show that the Philippines had fallen but the Filipino people have not and shall never bow their heads in submission to the rule of a nation which used nothing but brute force and inhuman deeds upon a conquered people. The fall of Bataan was the commencing date of the guerilla organization in Bataan and it marked the guerilla warfare against the Japanese that would become a menace to their occupation throughout the war.

Propaganda poster used outside of the occupied Philippines during the war, to bring awareness to the role of Filipino guerrillas.
National Park Service

troops as possible in their own "occupied" territory, thus keeping them out of their own front lines.

Marking often left Yay in charge of their main base while he took a steady stream of new recruits into the jungles for training.

Yay repeatedly warned Marking not to get himself killed needlessly in hopeless rescue operations or ill-planned attacks. "You are the brain of your fighters," she would say. "Who teaches them to spot the enemy and outthink them? Who keeps their morale up? . . . Who knows more about guns than you? And who do they look to more than to you?"

Marking knew Yay was right, and he often followed her advice. But sometimes getting him to listen took enormous effort. One day a guide named Pascual was brought into the camp by a guerrilla who accused him of working with the Japanese. Marking immediately ordered his execution.

Yay knew the accused man. He had once risked his life to hide some Americans. His wife had sheltered Yay. The present evidence against him was circumstantial and weak.

"We'll kill him for betrayal," said Marking.

"You'll *prove betrayal* first," replied Yay.

"Prepare a firing squad," said Marking.

"You *can't* kill him, Marking," said Yay.

"I *will* kill him," he insisted, pulling out his .45 pistol.

Yay stood next to the condemned man. "Then shoot us both," she said.

The other guerrillas moved slowly out of the line of fire. It was silent. Yay and Marking stared steadily at each other. Neither one would back down. Marking wanted to prove he was in charge. Yay wanted him to be reasonable and just.

Finally, Marking gave in. "You know I can't shoot you. *I love you.*"

This incident became a legend among Marking's guerrillas: Yay had openly challenged Marking and won. And when she knew him better, and discovered that his sense of justice was even sharper than her own, Yay realized he might have been bluffing, testing Pascual.

But even Yay was not opposed to taking a life when necessary. The occasional discovery of a genuine traitor was clear grounds for execution: to free them would sentence the entire unit to death. In these situations, however, Yay would order the men to kill quickly and humanely. She did this not only out of a sense of humanity for the condemned traitors but also for the sake of the guerrillas, in order to prevent them from being permanently "scarred by their own brutalities."

Although Yay didn't engage in the same physical exertion as the fighters, her own work exhausted her: "I was a one-woman staff," she wrote later. She did whatever needed doing: not only all the paperwork "but the hours after three a.m. when Marking talked, insisting that I listen and I reminded him of things, encouraged him, tried to clarify things for him."

But in spite of her fatigue, Yay was determined to "fight to the end."

That determination would soon be severely tested. On January 3, 1943, the unit's lookout reported a group of Japanese soldiers fast approaching, led by a Filipino man they didn't recognize.

As they scrambled to evacuate, bullets began flying over their heads. Yay knew they'd been fired from Japanese guns: they had a different sound than the American guns used by the Filipinos.

The unit evacuated in time and made a different camp. But the Japanese eventually discovered them there too. For months, they were on the run, going from camp to camp, always one step ahead of the enemy, fighting them as they traveled. Dangerously low on food and ammunition, Marking's guerrillas were often forced to ask villagers for help.

But they were not always welcome. The Japanese would brutally punish an entire village if they suspected that just one of its residents had helped a guerrilla: once, after Marking's guerrillas had rested in a certain village, they found it burned to the ground on the following day.

So they traveled away from the villages, away from any possible battles with the Japanese. "To leave them," Yay wrote, "was to save them."

They finally found a place to rest and regroup far from civilization, among some Filipinos called the Dumagats. One day, while among the Dumagats, a barefoot, gaunt American named Andy walked into their camp. His real name was Captain Bernard L. Anderson. He was one of many American guerrilla leaders in the Philippines during this time, some of whom had purposely sneaked behind enemy lines during the Battle of Bataan, with MacArthur's blessing, in order to engage in acts of sabotage; some who were cut off from their units during the fighting; some who were sent to the Philippines by submarine after the fall of Bataan and Corregidor; and a miraculous few who escaped at the beginning of the Bataan Death March or from prison camps.

Many of these Americans were discovered by Filipinos who requested they organize and lead them against the Japanese. Andy was one of these Americans approached by Filipinos, and his eventual band of 7,000 guerrillas focused on intelligence work. He wanted to authorize Marking to provide intelligence for the US military.

"I don't need to be authorized to fight for my own country!" Marking shouted. "Nobody has to give me permission to fight. I'd like to see anybody stop me! I'd like to see MacArthur stop me!"

★★

THE FILIPINO GUERRILLAS AND
THE RETURN OF MACARTHUR

General MacArthur had to convince President Franklin Roosevelt to let him keep his earlier promise to return to the Philippines. But Roosevelt was hesitant to initiate an invasion that might prove costly in terms of American lives. MacArthur persuaded him that the numerous Filipino guerrilla units would provide enough intelligence on the whereabouts of the Japanese military to ensure a successful invasion. When the president agreed, MacArthur sent urgent word to the Americans working with Filipino guerrillas, telling them to be prepared to take orders from him.

★★

Andy let Marking go on like this for a while, listening patiently, respectfully. Then he said, simply, "Authorization means bullets."

Marking's tone suddenly changed. He and Andy talked for a while. Finally, Andy asked, "Will you take orders from MacArthur?"

"Yes, but not from anybody else!" Marking replied.

"I will merely relay the orders," said Andy, smiling.

Marking invited Andy to a dinner in his honor. Then he quietly directed Yay—who had listened to the entire interchange in silence—to hammer out the precise details of their agreement.

As the return of MacArthur drew near, Marking's guerrillas worked closely with the Americans, providing them with important information regarding Japanese troop movements, which proved invaluable in making MacArthur's return a military success. But in order to observe the Japanese, Marking's guerrillas had to be near them. The fighters were often in great danger, even more so by what occurred during the liberation: when the Japanese realized defeat was inevitable, they considered every civilian in Manila a spy. The Japanese burned, raped, and killed civilians in enormous numbers. Before Manila was in American control, 100,000 of its civilians were dead, including some who had been simply caught in crossfire.

However, most of Marking's unit managed to elude the enemy, sometimes by mere minutes and yards.

As the Japanese were being pushed out, Yay and Marking had a major disagreement. Yay decided to return to her parents' home in California to regain her health and to put some distance between herself and Marking. She wrote to Carlos Romulo that the war had "wrenched" her soul while exposing her "to every possible emotion" and had been "by far the stiffest test of the human character" she had yet endured.

While resting in California, she received dozens of letters from Marking and his fighters. The first was a "pledge" that read in part:

Whereas, This organization, "MARKING'S GUERRIL- LAS," had been duly inducted into the United States Army; . . .

Whereas, henceforth this regiment will be known and called the "YAY REGIMENT" in honor of our beloved guerilla mother . . . who nursed us, comforted us, bawled us out, and loved us all those years we were hiding in the hills and mountains, and pulled through despite hunger and starvation.

★★

BROKEN PROMISES AND THE RESCISSION ACT OF 1946

Approximately 250,000 Filipino fighters officially joined the US Army during World War II. They were promised full military benefits in return. But the Rescission Act of 1946 canceled that promise, except to the families of veterans who had died or been wounded in combat. The faulty reasoning behind the Rescission Act was this: because the Philippines was now completely independent from the United States and no longer a US colony (1898–1935) or a US commonwealth nation (1935–1946), the Philippine government should provide for its own veterans. But the war had devastated the Philippine economy.

In 2009, the Filipino Veterans Equity Compensation Fund was organized to provide Filipino World War II veterans with at least the possibility of claiming some financial compensation, in the form of modest one-time payments. While 18,000 such claims have been approved, not all attempts to access these payments have been successful.

★★

After the war, Yay and Marking were married and spent their immediate postwar years in the Philippines, working tirelessly to gain official recognition for Marking's guerrillas. With this in mind, Yay wrote her memoir in 1950, gearing it for American readers unacquainted with the enormous Filipino contribution to the war effort. Later that year she received the Medal of Freedom from the US government for her wartime work.

Yay's marriage to Marking didn't last, and she returned to the United States in the 1970s when martial law was imposed in the Philippines.

She died in New York City in 1978.

LEARN MORE

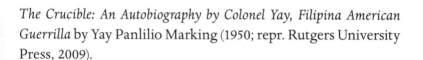

The Crucible: An Autobiography by Colonel Yay, Filipina American Guerrilla by Yay Panlilio Marking (1950; repr. Rutgers University Press, 2009).

I Saw the Fall of the Philippines by Carlos P. Romulo (Doubleday, 1944).

I See the Philippines Rise by Carlos P. Romulo (Doubleday, 1946).

Lieutenant Ramsey's War: From Horse Soldier to Guerrilla Commander by Edwin Price Ramsey and Stephen J. Rivele (Brassey's, 1990).

CLAIRE PHILLIPS

Manila Agent

A GLITTERING PARADE of Japanese elite crowded into the Tsubaki Club on its opening night: film stars, famous musicians, military officers, and civilian officials. None of them wanted to miss the first night of Manila's new, most exclusive nightclub.

The guests were treated to one dazzling dance production after another. For the finale, the elegant owner appeared alone on the dance floor. Dressed in a long, glittering white evening gown, Dorothy Fuentes sang beautifully for her guests. When she was finished, the crowd jumped to their feet in a thunderous standing ovation.

When the last guests had left, Dorothy checked the overflowing cash box. She knew that the Tsubaki Club was now the most popular spot for the Japanese in Manila. Her plan would work.

She wrote the following note: "Our new show was a sell out. You can count on regular backing. Standing by for orders and assignments."

Claire Phillips, 1940s. Manila Espionage *by Claire Phillips and Myron B. Goldsmith (Binfords & Mort, 1947)*

She was about to sign it, then stopped. She couldn't use her name; it was too risky. But what could she use as an alias? She thought for a moment about how she always stashed money in her bra. She signed the note, "High Pockets."

The woman's real name was Claire Phillips. She had been born Mabel Clara Dela Taste in 1907 in Michigan but went by Claire. She left home at the age of 16 and traveled throughout the United States for more than a decade, working various jobs as a vaudeville actress and chorus girl. When Claire was in her early 30s, she landed in Manila, where she eventually got work singing in Manila nightclubs.

One night in September 1941, an American serviceman named Private John V. Phillips, whom everyone called Phil, saw her perform. As rumors of war swirled throughout the Philippines, Claire and Phil began a whirlwind courtship. On December 24, 1941, a few weeks after the war rumors had become reality, they held a formal ceremony in which they pledged to marry as soon as they could. Although they were not yet married, Claire took Phil's last name.

As the US and Filipino troops evacuated Manila for the Bataan Peninsula, Phil found a place for Claire to stay outside of the city. Manila would no longer be safe for American or European civilians: the Japanese were coming. As one living situation after another became unsafe for Claire, Phil always found a way to get away and move her to safety. In the meantime, Claire began to tan herself in the sun; with darker skin and her already dark hair, she could pretend to be someone else, someone who wasn't an American, an enemy of Imperial Japan.

Then she lost contact with Phil. One day, as she searched for news of him, she was told that three American soldiers, separated from their regiment, were being sheltered nearby.

Claire rushed to meet them. She asked if they knew the whereabouts of a John Phillips who had been with their regiment, the 31st Infantry. They didn't: the 31st Infantry was large.

But one of them, a man named John Boone, had an idea: creating a guerrilla band of Filipino soldiers.

"So why don't you set it up?" Claire asked him.

"Only one reason," Boone answered. "Supplies. We need a contact in Manila. And that could be you!"

It was an excellent idea. Claire could see Boone was a natural leader, and she knew there were many Filipino civilians willing to fight the Japanese if given the opportunity. As soon as word got out to them, an effective unit could be formed.

"We won't stand and give battle," Boone continued, "but kill the Japs one by one."

Claire left, her mind spinning with ideas. But her focus was still on Phil. Where was he? One day she learned that he had been imprisoned in Manila. Now she had two reasons to return there: John Boone's plan and her husband. Dressed in men's clothing, Claire made the difficult journey to Manila.

But when she arrived, she discovered Phil had been taken elsewhere. She decided to stop searching for him. By this time, the Americans and the Filipinos on Bataan and Corregidor had surrendered to the Japanese. Now was the time for a different sort of war, a secret one in which Claire could actively participate. She could fight this battle most effectively in Manila. She would fight for the oppressed Filipino people. She would fight for John Boone and his guerrilla band. And she would fight for Phil, wherever he was.

Her first step was crucial: a new identity. Claire was now so tanned, she could easily pass for an Italian or Spaniard. She chose Italian as she didn't think most Japanese were familiar with the language or culture. She obtained some official-looking papers declaring her to be Dorothy Clara Fuentes, an Italian native who had become a Filipino citizen.

On October 17, 1942, Claire opened a nightclub located near Manila's busy harbor. She named it the Tsubaki Club after a rare Japanese flower. Her opening night was a huge success, and she looked forward to earning more Japanese money to fund resistance efforts. But her mind was always on Phil.

The following day, Claire felt the time was right to get an update on him. She called on Father Theodore Buttenbruch, a fellow resister and German priest who the Japanese were allowing to visit Cabanatuan under careful supervision. She asked Father Buttenbruch if he would carry a message to Phil.

Two weeks later, the priest called Claire to his office. He had lists of POWs who had died at Cabanatuan. Phil had died, he said, on July 26, 1942.

A few days later, she received a sympathy note from Chaplain Frank Tiffany, who lived at Cabanatuan. Although Phil's death certificate stated that he had died of malaria, Chaplain Tiffany told Claire the underlying reason for Phil's death was malnutrition.

"But I beg of you," he continued, "not to forget the ones that are left. They are dying by the hundreds."

Claire was heartbroken. It took her several days to recover enough to return to work. But when she did, the circumstances of Phil's death gave her an additional motivation to keep the Tsubaki Club successful. She also became more motivated to engage in her own form of espionage.

The Tsubaki Club regularly entertained powerful Japanese civilians and military men who passed through Manila. Claire focused most of her attention on the military men: she or one of the other women would flirt with them while encouraging them to drink. The alcohol would often get them talking freely about where they had been and where they were going.

One night, a Japanese officer who commanded an entire flotilla of submarines visited the Tsubaki Club. A club employee told Claire the man was a great admirer of her singing. Claire, flirting and smiling, joined him at his table. He didn't drink much and talked even less. This wasn't going to be easy.

Suddenly, he told Claire that he liked her and hoped the feeling was mutual. He was sad that he would soon be leaving Manila. Then he asked her if she could dance as well as she could sing.

"You should have to be the judge of that, Commander," Claire answered. "I am so disappointed you must leave. Not immediately, I hope."

"Tomorrow afternoon, I finish repairs on our submarines," he replied. He said he would be willing to delay just a little, however, if Claire would perform a fan dance (for which the dancer wore a costume that made her appear naked).

After obliging the commander with her dance, Claire had someone "photograph" the two of them with an empty camera. Where should she send the photos once developed, she asked.

That would be impossible, he said. He and his flotilla were on their way to the Solomon Islands.

Claire calmly excused herself long enough to write a note with the information she had just been given. A courier took the note and immediately set out for John Boone's camp.

When she returned to the officer's table, Claire and her female employees drank, flirted, and danced with him and his men all night. The officer, having a good time with Claire, often glanced at his wristwatch, asking her to please keep track of the time; he had to leave by 2:00 AM.

Claire did nothing of the sort. She and her staff delayed them till after 6:00 AM, long enough for the note to reach John Boone and for him to radio it to USAFFE headquarters in Australia.

A few months later, the same Japanese commander returned to the Tsubaki Club. He told Claire, sadly, that his flotilla had been attacked and most of it destroyed. He survived only because he was picked up by a fishing boat.

Claire's earnings were already funding Margaret Utinsky's Miss U Network (chapter 6). But after December 1942, when Margaret, distraught from news of her husband's death, became less involved in her network, Claire, with the help of Spanish businessman Ramon Amusategui, gradually took some control of the network. Under their leadership and funding, the organization grew larger and became even more successful at funneling medicine and food into Cabanatuan and other prison camps outside and within Manila.

One of their plans fed the starving Cabanatuan prisoners right under the noses of the Japanese: on the days when the prisoners were allowed to visit the nearby market, members of the network posing as vendors would "sell" the Americans parcels of food that had money and medicine hidden inside.

Claire was so determined to help the Americans, she decided to take an even more direct role. Clara Yuma, known as Claring, the aunt of one of Claire's waiters, told her nephew about an American crew of slave laborers being forced to work at the Nichols Airfield. Every day the prisoners walked on a certain road from their prison camp. When Claire learned of this, she and Claring watched them one day from an abandoned shack on the route.

Describing the scene later, Claire wrote that on seeing the gaunt prisoners, her "heart sank." She found it difficult to believe that "these ragged [men] with shaven heads and red-ringed eyes were once proud American fighting men." As they "stumbled along the uneven gravel road," Claire was further horrified by their "cut and bleeding bare feet" and the "big festering sores on their legs," most likely the result of malnutrition and untreated illnesses.

Claire's compassion propelled her into action. She rented a house in Claring's name along the route, and they both set up a shed across the street. Claring became friendly with the Japanese guards who escorted the prisoners. Claire was too well known in Manila, so she watched from inside the house. Claring bribed the Japanese guards with gifts so they would allow her to give the prisoners food packets, which Claire had funded and both women had prepared.

As the weeks passed, the prisoners not only began to look healthier, but the despair on their faces was gone, replaced with a glimmer of hope.

After four months, however, the Japanese guards suddenly became dissatisfied with their gifts. One of them slapped Claring repeatedly in front of the prisoners, who were helpless to intervene. The guards then forced her to shut down the food stand. But others in the network continued to help the same men in other, secretive ways, always funded by Claire's earnings from the Tsubaki Club.

Claire invited the Manila resistance to use her club as a secret headquarters. Agents walked in and out in a variety of disguises: repairmen, milkmen, meter readers, and peddlers. No one outside the network seemed to be aware of their real identities. That was about to change.

During the summer of 1943, a guerrilla courier code-named CIO-12 was caught. After long, agonizing days of horrific torture at the hands of the Kempeitai, he finally broke down and disclosed information. The Japanese immediately executed him, then convinced a Filipino con man to take on his identity. The imposter gained the trust of enough people, who, of course, hadn't known the original agent. Soon the resistance network headquartered at the Tsubaki Club was infiltrated. One by one, its members began falling into the hands of the Kempeitai.

One morning, a young Filipino man who claimed to be a courier handed Claire a letter from an American named Captain Bagley. The letter was a request to fund a group of Filipino guerrillas.

Claire immediately knew the message was fake. It was written in a formal style not used by any Americans she knew. And the young man had not given any proper identification.

She responded angrily, claiming to be an Italian who didn't care about the Americans or the guerrillas.

As the young man left, Claire signaled one of the waiters to follow him. The waiter returned with a chilling report: the "courier" had been met by four Japanese men in civilian clothing. Claire was obviously under suspicion.

Her friends urged her to flee to the guerrillas in the mountains. She refused. She didn't believe the Japanese seriously suspected her of espionage. If so, why hadn't they arrested her already? Plus—and this was crucial—how could she provide information and money to the resistance if she was in hiding? But as a precaution, she cleared her office of any incriminating documents that might cast doubt on her false identity.

During the following months, as Claire worked tirelessly against the Japanese, the Kempeitai continued to close in on the network. On May 23, 1944, Kempeitai agents stormed into the Tsubaki Club. *"Jitto shita cri!"* ["Don't move!"] one of them shouted.

They searched Claire to see if she was carrying a weapon.

"You are Madame Tsubaki?" they asked.

"Yes," Claire replied.

"Take us to your office, High-Pockets!"

Claire was terrified: they knew who she was. As they searched her office, she tried not to tremble as she recalled all she'd heard about the horrific tortures the Kempeitai used to extract information.

Although they didn't find anything incriminating, the Kempeitai agents shoved Claire into a car and drove her to the Japanese administration building a few blocks away. They put her in a tiny room, blindfolded her, then interrogated her about others in the network. She answered "I don't know" to almost every question. Each time she said those words, she received a vicious slap across the face or a hard kick to her shins.

After two weeks, she was moved to Fort Santiago, where she was imprisoned in a filthy cell, measuring 7 by 12 feet, with six other women.

During her imprisonment, Claire endured grueling torture that, on multiple occasions, threatened her very sanity. But on her return from every interrogation, the other women did their best to help her recover some strength.

On February 10, 1945, nearly nine months after her initial arrest, Claire was liberated by American troops. The already slim woman had lost 55 pounds while in captivity. She hadn't betrayed anyone.

Claire wrote her memoir in 1947, and the following year she was awarded with the US Presidential Medal of Freedom. In 1951, her memoir was made into a highly fictionalized film called *I Was an American Spy*.

Suffering severely from untreated posttraumatic stress, Claire died of alcoholism-related meningitis in 1960 at the age of 52.

LEARN MORE

——————— ★ ———————

Angels of the Underground: The American Women who Resisted the Japanese in the Philippines in World War II by Theresa Kaminski (New York: Oxford, 2016).

Ghost Soldiers: The Epic Account of World War II's Greatest Rescue Mission by Hampton Sides (Random House, 2001). Contains a section on Claire Phillips.

Manila Espionage by Claire Phillips and Myron B. Goldsmith (Binfords & Mort, 1947); republished as *Agent High Pockets: A Woman's Fight Against the Japanese in the Philippines* (Uncommon Valor, 2014), Kindle e-book.

"Manila Mata Hari" by Brian Libby, *Portland Monthly*, January 14, 2011, www.pdxmonthly.com/articles/2011/1/14/ana-fey-january-2011.

MARIA ROSA HENSON

Guerrilla Courier and Rape Survivor

WHEN 14-YEAR-OLD Filipina Maria Rosa approached her school in Pasay, near Manila, on December 8, 1941, she noticed something unusual: the students were standing outside instead of going in. Why? The school was closed. Japan had attacked the Philippines.

Maria Rosa and her mother fled with some neighbors to a small village farther north on Luzon, the main island of the Philippines. Life had always been difficult for Maria Rosa, the unacknowledged daughter of a rich, already married father and the single young woman he had pressured into becoming his mistress. Maria Rosa and her mother had always lived near poverty, but now, during the Japanese occupation, survival became even more difficult.

After returning to Pasay, Maria Rosa heard there was firewood available at nearby Fort McKinley, a former US military base now being used by the Japanese. One day, after a week of

Self-portrait of Maria Rosa as a schoolgirl in 1941. *Comfort Woman: A Filipina's Story of Prostitution and Slavery Under the Japanese Military by Maria Rosa Henson (Rowman & Littlefield, 1999)*

collecting the bundles of firewood, on her way back from Fort McKinley, Maria Rosa suddenly came face-to-face with two Japanese soldiers. They grabbed her arms. She cried out. While she struggled to get free, a Japanese officer approached them. He yelled something in Japanese at the soldiers. Then he slapped them. Maria Rosa was relieved: she thought he was going to rescue her.

Instead, he raped her. Then he allowed the two soldiers to rape her as well, before walking away. Maria Rosa's skirt was covered with blood. She was in so much pain, she couldn't get up. A kind farmer who happened to pass by carried her home to his wife. She gave Maria Rosa a different set of clothes and cared for her until she felt well enough to walk home.

When Maria Rosa's mother heard what had happened, she tried to prevent her from returning to the fort. But because they needed the wood, Maria Rosa returned without her mother's permission, this time accompanied by her uncles and neighbors. Certainly, she thought, being in a large group would offer her protection.

It didn't. When they all arrived at the fort, Maria Rosa saw the officer who had raped her. He recognized her, and in full view of her uncles, who were helpless to intervene, he raped her again.

Maria Rosa's horrified mother was determined to leave the area. They moved to her home village of Pampang (in the Pampanga province), where they shared a house with a male relative by the name of Pinatubo. He was a commander in the Hukbalahap, a Communist-based Filipino guerrilla army referred to as the Huk.

One day Pinatubo asked Maria Rosa if she wanted to join the Huk. She was glad to be offered a chance to fight back against the Japanese. After joining, she was assigned to carry messages and collect food, medicine, and clothing from people sympathetic to the Huk guerrillas.

Once, while on her way to collect medicine and deliver a message, Maria Rosa saw some Japanese soldiers a long way off. She quickly ate the message. The soldiers suspected nothing and let her pass.

But Maria Rosa knew she'd had a close call. Those suspected of working with the Huk were always taken to the local Japanese garrison, where they were tortured for information before being killed. So the Huk held their meetings in different neighborhoods in order to avoid detection. And as Maria Rosa went from village to village for the Huk, she was careful to never disclose her real identity: her code name was Bayang.

Maria Rosa's work gave her a deep sense of purpose. Yet she was continually haunted by the memory of the rapes, especially when she sang the following lines of a song with her comrades:

They should be vanquished, the fascist Japanese,
The scourge of our race.
They seized our possessions and raped our women.

After singing those words, Maria Rosa would always whisper to herself, "I am one of those women."

One morning in April, 1943, Maria Rosa and two male comrades, riding in a cart pulled by a carabao (a type of water buffalo), approached a Japanese checkpoint. The cart looked like it was filled with sacks of corn, but some of the sacks also contained ammunition and weapons.

Maria Rosa showed the Japanese sentry their passes. He touched some of the corn sacks. Then he allowed them to move on.

But before they got far from the checkpoint, the sentry whistled and signaled for them to return. "We looked at each other and turned pale," Maria Rosa wrote later. "If he emptied the sack, he would surely find the guns and kill us instantly."

A Hukbalahap meeting. Sketch by Maria Rosa Henson. Comfort Woman: A Filipina's Story of Prostitution and Slavery Under the Japanese Military *by Maria Rosa Henson (Rowman & Littlefield, 1999)*

Then the sentry pointed to her: she was the only one who needed to return.

"I walked to the checkpoint, thinking the guns were safe but I would be in danger. I thought that maybe they would rape me."

At gunpoint, the sentry led Maria Rosa to the second floor of a Japanese garrison. There she saw six other women. She was led a small room with a bamboo bed and no door, only a curtain.

On the following day, one that she would later describe as "hell," Maria Rosa discovered why she and the other women had been brought to the garrison. A Japanese soldier entered her room. He pointed a bayonet at her chest. She was terrified; she thought he was going to kill her. Instead, he slashed her dress open. Then he raped her.

★★

FILIPINA COMFORT WOMEN

Most of the approximately 200,000 so-called comfort women who were enslaved in "comfort stations" (in reality rape stations) by the Japanese military throughout Asia during World War II were lured by false promises of regular work. But in the Philippines, because the Philippine resistance movement was so strong and Japanese troops stationed there regarded most civilians as being possible resisters, the Japanese usually abducted women and girls openly. By early 1943 in Manila alone there were 17 rape stations for soldiers, "staffed" by 1,064 enslaved women, and four officers' clubs served by 120.

★★

Twelve more soldiers followed.

When it was over, Maria Rosa was in extreme pain and bleeding profusely. Another woman brought some food in the morning, but Maria Rosa wasn't allowed to talk to her. There was a guard by the door to prevent not only escape but conversation as well; the Japanese had isolated these women, in part, to prevent them from engaging in any espionage while in contact with the Japanese military men.

From then on, Maria was raped repeatedly every day and often beaten during the process. "At the end of each day," she wrote later, "I just closed my eyes and cried." She couldn't see any way out. She knew that an escape attempt would mean death. Only love for her mother kept her from suicide.

At one point the women were transferred from the garrison to a rice mill that a new set of officers had taken over. One of them was the officer who had raped Maria Rosa outside of Fort McKinley the year before. His name was Captain Tanka. He recognized Maria

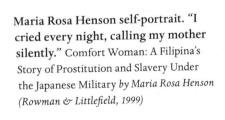

Maria Rosa Henson self-portrait. "I cried every night, calling my mother silently." Comfort Woman: A Filipina's Story of Prostitution and Slavery Under the Japanese Military *by Maria Rosa Henson (Rowman & Littlefield, 1999)*

Rosa and took pity on her several times when she became ill with malaria, allowing her to recover in his own room, usually without raping her. She was beginning to learn some Japanese, and Tanka had learned some English. One day she pleaded with him to help her escape. He refused, saying that doing so would break his vow to serve the emperor. And "he could do nothing against the Emperor."

One day, Tanka asked Maria Rosa to bring tea to his room. When she entered, she found him in conversation with a Japanese colonel. They were discussing plans to burn Pampang to the ground in retaliation for suspected guerrilla activities there. Maria Rosa knew that when the Japanese burned a village, they also set up their machine guns around the outside so they could fire on anyone who managed to escape the flames. Her village was doomed!

She was determined to alert Pampang. She found her opportunity on the following day. When the guards let the women out for some sunshine, Maria Rosa went as close to the street as the barbed wire would allow. She saw an old Filipino man walk by. She knew he lived in Pampang. The guards were distracted, laughing and talking together. They didn't see her whisper a warning to the old man.

That evening she saw Captain Tanka and the colonel leave with some soldiers. When they returned one hour later, the two officers rushed up the stairs to her room. The colonel slapped her viciously. Why? They had found Pampang deserted. Maria Rosa was the only civilian who could have possibly overheard their plans.

She was dragged to the basement, beaten, and tied up. When she dared to open her eyes and look around, she recognized some Huk guerrillas, also bound with rope, their bodies and faces covered with bruises.

Captain Tanka came down and tried to give Maria Rosa some tea. But the colonel stopped him. Then he banged Maria Rosa's head against the iron wall. She lost consciousness.

That night, Huk guerrillas attacked the garrison in order to save their comrades. They also rescued the unconscious Maria Rosa. She was eventually taken to her mother's house.

When she regained consciousness, she couldn't walk or even sit up. She couldn't speak. Her mouth constantly hung open. Her vision was blurry. She tried to write down what she was experiencing but couldn't hold the pencil. Her mother had to care for her as if she were a baby.

As she regained her ability to speak, Maria Rosa told her mother what the Japanese soldiers had done to her. Her mother wouldn't allow her outside for almost a year for fear the Japanese soldiers would recognize her and take her back.

When they heard the news that Manila was liberated, everyone was overjoyed. But Maria couldn't stop crying; tears not of joy but of sorrow that the Americans had come too late to save her from her ordeal. She was continuously tormented, not only by her horrific memories but because she hadn't tried to escape.

Maria Rosa recovered enough to marry Domingo, a kind Filipino soldier who had been a guerrilla during the war. She didn't tell him about the full extent of her ordeal, but she did admit she'd been raped by Japanese soldiers. He loved her and said that her past didn't matter. They had three children together.

Their marriage ended when Domingo was abducted by a group of Filipino guerrillas who had been Communist Huks during the war. After the war, when General Douglas MacArthur arrested Huk leaders and ordered their followers to disband, many escaped to the mountains with their weapons. There they tried to fight against wealthy landlords who had fled to urban areas during the war and were now demanding back rent from their war-impoverished tenants, many of them former guerrilla fighters who had lost everything. Domingo stayed with these guerrillas, became their leader, and took another wife.

Now on her own, Maria Rosa went to work in a factory and used her earnings to ensure that her children and grandchildren each received an education. She didn't tell anyone about what happened to her during the war.

Then one morning in 1992, she heard a woman on the radio discussing the topic of so-called comfort women who had been forced into sexual slavery by the Japanese government during the war.

Maria Rosa began to shake uncontrollably. She heard the woman on the radio discuss something called the Task Force on Filipino Comfort Women. "Don't be ashamed," the woman said. "Being a sex slave is not your fault. It is the responsibility of the Japanese Imperial Army. Stand up and fight for your rights."

"My heart was beating very fast," Maria wrote later of that moment. "I asked myself whether I should expose my ordeal. What if my children and relatives found me dirty and repulsive?"

She didn't call in, but she listened to that radio station every day. A few weeks later, she heard a similar announcement. She began to weep. At that moment, her daughter Rosario walked in. Maria Rosa finally told her the truth.

Rosario helped her get in touch with the task force. Maria Rosa was interviewed on tape, Rosario at her side. It was extremely difficult, but also a relief. "I felt like a heavy weight had been removed from my shoulders," she wrote later, "as if thorns had been pulled out of my grieving heart. I felt I had recovered my long-lost strength and self-esteem."

Maria Rosa was the first Filipina comfort woman to break her silence. The task force now asked her to take a more public stance. She couldn't refuse. "There were others, like me," she wrote later, "and they, like me, needed to have a measure of justice before they died. I also wanted to make the younger generation aware about the evils of war."

She gave press conferences and made radio appearances. And later that year, she met other former Filipina comfort women. Her efforts eventually inspired a total of 168 former Filipina sex slaves to come forward.

In April 1993, with Maria Rosa in the lead, 18 former Filipina comfort women officially filed a lawsuit against the Japanese government, demanding an official apology and some money for each woman. Testifying in Japanese court was extremely strenuous for these older women who had waited so long to tell their stories.

While waiting for the court case to go through, Maria Rosa wrote her memoir. She was able to recall many details because she had "learned to remember everything, to remember always, so [she would] not go mad." She wanted to tell her story, she said, so that the Japanese rapists would "feel humiliated."

The Japanese government insisted it owed the women nothing since it had already paid some postwar reparations to the Philippine government. However, with increased pressure to acknowledge the former sex slaves of many Asian nations, the Japanese government allowed the creation of the Asian Women's Fund. Maria eventually accepted a $19,000 settlement from this fund, a move that was criticized by some who thought she should have waited for direct compensation from the Japanese government.

With her settlement money, Maria Rosa bought a small house in Manila. She died there in August 1997.

LEARN MORE

Comfort Woman: A Filipina's Story of Prostitution and Slavery Under the Japanese Military by Maria Rosa Henson (Rowman & Littlefield, 1999).

Comfort Women: Sexual Slavery in the Japanese Military During World War II by Yoshimi Yoshiaki (Columbia University Press, 1995).

50 Years of Silence: Comfort Woman of Indonesia by Jan Ruff-O'Herne (Editions Tom Thompson, 1994).

PART III

Malaya, Singapore, and the Dutch East Indies

SYBIL KATHIGASU

"This Was War"

ON DECEMBER 8, 1941, one of Sybil Kathigasu's neighbors popped his head inside her door. "Have you heard the news, Mrs. K?" he cried. "It's war! The Japanese have bombed Singapore!"

Sybil—"Mrs. K."—was not surprised by this report. But it still filled her with a cold dread she tried to hide from the rest of her family. She wanted to be a source of strength for her physician husband, her elderly mother, and her three children, who all lived together in a house at the center of Ipoh, a bustling Malayan town.

During the next few days, Sybil—a nurse and midwife—was encouraged by the stream of military convoys she saw pass through Ipoh's streets, their trucks loaded with Malayan soldiers heading north to fight the Japanese who had landed there.

After they had gone, Ipoh became so quiet, its residents could almost imagine Malaya was not at war. That would soon be impossible. On December 15, while traveling north of Ipoh to

Sybil Kathigasu before the war.
Media Masters Publishing, Malaysia

visit a patient, Sybil noticed planes circling high off in the distance. Her driver said they must be British Royal Air Force planes.

They weren't. When she was finished attending her patient, Sybil was told that the Japanese had just bombed Ipoh.

She returned to a devastated town and a wounded husband. His wounds were not life-threatening, however, and he was quickly discharged into her care. Sybil drove him and the rest of her family to a small structure away from the center of Ipoh, where she hoped they might be safe, out of the range of the Japanese bombers.

When the Kathigasu family emerged a few days later, several things were quite clear. The war was going badly for the Malayan forces in the north; the Japanese were pushing them south. There was no longer any reason for the Kathigasus to stay in Ipoh; it was deserted, and nearly all their patients had fled.

They joined the throngs of refugees fleeing south, until they came to a little village called Papan. They found a small house on the town's only street and opened a medical clinic there as well.

The Japanese entered Papan on December 28. Their occupation was brutal. The soldiers raped so many Malayan girls that Sybil made her 20-year-old daughter Olga dress as a man. Many less fortunate young women were raped and abducted, never to be heard from again.

The occupying Japanese administration forced the Malayans to abandon Western culture and replace it with Japanese. Malayans had their homes searched regularly to ensure no one still owned pictures of the British royal family, the flags of any Allied nations, or even American record albums.

The Japanese were also obsessed with persecuting Papan's large Chinese population. They would randomly round them up and make them stand for hours—sometimes days—in the hot sun without food or water. Many collapsed, and some died.

A guerrilla movement was born out of this persecution. The Chinese guerrillas near Papan fought the Japanese occupation by assassinating Malayan collaborators who were betraying their fellow Malayans to the Japanese. Large Japanese offensives would then be launched against the guerrillas. But when collaborators continued to meet their doom from hidden assassins, everyone knew the guerrillas were, in the main, alive and well.

One day, they asked Sybil for help.

"It's the guerillas, Mrs. K," said Moru, a young Chinese man acquainted with her. "Some of them are sick and wounded, and need medicines. They knew you don't like the Japs. Will you help?"

Sybil knew the Japanese penalty for helping a guerrilla was severe. If she agreed to help them, she would be endangering not only herself but her beloved family. She already possessed a radio with which she regularly listened to the BBC (British Broadcasting Corporation), another highly illegal activity in Japanese-occupied Malaya. How much should she risk?

She told Moru to come back in an hour; she would have some medicine ready.

"I could not approve of some of the guerillas' methods," she wrote later, explaining her decision, "but this was war."

Moru became the link between Sybil and the guerrillas. Because he had been training as a teacher before the war, his declared reason for being at the Kathigasu home so often was to tutor Sybil's five-year-old daughter, Dawn.

The always crowded clinic was the perfect place for the guerrillas to come for mild to moderate ailments or with requests for information, messages, or warnings. The guerrillas, dressed as farmers, did not stand out in the crowd. And because Sybil spoke several Chinese dialects, there was nothing to arouse the suspicions of collaborators on seeing her in constant conversation with Chinese villagers.

One day Sybil received an urgent message from Moru: a guerrilla had been severely wounded, shot twice. One of the bullets, lodged in his ankle, was causing a painful inflammation resulting in a high fever. He was so sick he, would be unable to blend in easily with the other clinic patients. And he needed much more than medicine; unless someone operated on him immediately, he would certainly die. Because the Japanese had ordered all bullet-wound cases reported immediately, taking him to a hospital was out of the question: the penalty for operating on such a wound without reporting it was death.

Sybil wasn't a surgeon. Her husband was. But even if she could convince him to take the case, how could the wounded man access the clinic? The roads were always guarded by

Japanese sentries, and especially so after a clash with the Chinese guerrillas.

Transportation, Moru said, would not be a problem. But would Dr. Kathigasu perform the operation?

Sybil wasn't sure. But she would ask him. She drove to Ipoh and told her husband he was needed in Papan the following evening.

"Very well, 'Bil," Dr. Kathigasu said to his wife. "What sort of case is it?"

"Bullet wounds, received in a battle with the Japs."

"What about the risk, 'Bil?" he asked, clearly shocked. "You know I'm thinking about the children."

Sybil explained precautions that would be taken: the guerrillas would bring the man after dark, when the local sentries had left the area. The men would enter through the back door, an entrance hidden by high garden walls. Then they would make their presence known by three quiet taps on the door.

Dr. Kathigasu agreed to take the case. On the following evening, about 8:00 PM, quiet knocks were heard at the back door. Two armed Chinese men carried a very sick man inside. One of the men stayed with the patient while the other kept watch outside.

Removing the bullets was difficult and time-consuming—Sybil helped her husband locate the bullet amid the man's shattered ankle bone fragments—but the operation was a success. The guerrilla recovered at the foot of the mountains in a hut and was taken to the clinic every day for treatment. His companions told curious neighbors that he was from a distant farm and had been suffering from a fever.

After that, a steady stream of seriously wounded guerrillas was brought to the clinic. The local police in Papan were clearly on Sybil's side: they would often appear near her house at 7:00

PM, behaving as if they were seriously patrolling the area, but they always left long before 8:00 PM, when the wounded guerrillas would arrive.

Sybil tried to keep the knowledge of what they were doing from Dawn. And since her little daughter was usually in bed when the guerrillas arrived, it wasn't a problem. But then one evening, a horrified Sybil found Dawn in the back room, sitting on the lap of a guerrilla and playing with his empty revolver and bullets.

"What are these for, Mummy?" she asked innocently.

Sybil felt compelled to tell her daughter what was going on. "All those men who come here are soldiers who are sick and need medicine. They are fighting to save us from the Japs. . . . Nobody must know they are here. If somebody sees them come here, he might tell the Japs and these soldiers will be shot.

"If you love me, you must promise never to say a word about what you have seen here. These men are fighting for us. Whatever happens, we must never let them be killed."

"I will never tell anybody," Dawn promised.

"That's Mummy's brave girl. . . . From now on you shall always help me and be the youngest soldier of all."

After that night, Sybil told Dawn everything, and the young girl charmed all of the guerrillas who visited the Kathigasu home.

One day Moru gave Sybil a serious warning: the Japanese were looking for a Chinese midwife who was apparently helping the guerrillas in the Papan area.

Sybil was not concerned. If they were looking for a Chinese woman, she was safe.

Moru disagreed. "They will learn the truth sooner or later," Moru said, "and you must not fall into their hands, Mrs. K. We ought to take precautions."

"We cannot avoid what is to be, Moru," Sybil answered before changing the subject.

A few days later, Sybil received a letter from guerrilla headquarters urging her to move with her family to the hills. Huts would be built for all of them in a safe area.

Sybil liked the idea, but she decided against it. For one, her elderly mother was too old to endure life in the hills. Also, if the whole family suddenly disappeared, the Japanese would know they had left to avoid Sybil's arrest and would certainly avenge themselves on the remaining Papan villagers.

She sent her refusal to headquarters. When the offer was repeated through a messenger, Sybil urged him to not worry about her anymore but instead concern himself with preparing his men for the day when the Japanese would finally be driven out of Malaya.

The messenger was silent. He took Dawn on his knee and stroked her curls thoughtfully. Then he said, "We are alive one day but may be dead the next."

"Yes," Sybil replied, "but if we die to win the freedom that others may enjoy, there is comfort in that."

A few days later, she was arrested.

The news spread quickly. A large crowd of concerned neighbors gathered around the Kathigasu home, where Sybil had been allowed to get ready before being escorted to police headquarters. Some of the neighbors who had come to say good-bye were Sybil's patients. She gave them extra medicine and instructions.

Moru approached her with an urgent message: the leader of the guerrillas was ready to ambush the police who were on their way to take Sybil away.

She was touched but again refused.

Just before 8:00 PM, two local constables came to arrest Sybil, apologizing profusely. They took her to Papan's police headquarters. An hour and a half later, 10 heavily armed and clearly nervous men arrived at the station to escort her to prison.

She was eventually taken to the Kempeitai headquarters just outside Ipoh, where the head of the area's Kempeitai, Sergeant Eko Yoshimura, interrogated her daily. He knew she'd had a radio, but his main concern was the whereabouts of the guerrillas. When her answers didn't satisfy him, he beat her viciously. She endured the beatings. She did not betray the guerrillas.

But Sergeant Yoshimura was determined to break her. One day he brought her outside and tied her to a pillar. Then he ordered an officer to fetch Dawn.

Sybil was frantic. "Officer, please leave Dawn out of this."

"You love your child, don't you?" he asked. "You can prove your love when she arrives."

When Dawn came, some officers tied her hands behind her back and a rope around her chest. They threatened to kill Dawn in front of Sybil.

"Speak!" Yoshimura shrieked. "Tell us all about the guerillas or we'll burn your daughter before your eyes. Speak! Speak! Speak!" He cracked Sybil over the head with his cane.

"Don't tell, Mummy," cried Dawn. "I love you and we'll die together."

"Is this the bravery of Dai Nippon ["the great Japanese"]," Sybil screamed, "to torture and kill a little child? I always thought the Japanese were cowards; now I know that it is true."

She was rewarded for her outburst with severe blows to her head. But she barely felt them because she was terrified for Dawn and desperately praying for a miracle.

Suddenly, all the Japanese stood at attention. An officer approached, obviously someone of senior rank. He gave a few short, sharp commands. One of the men freed Dawn, and someone untied Sybil. She rushed to embrace her child.

Then she waved her hand in the air and shouted, "Long live Malaya and the British!" She turned to Yoshimura: "You'll pay for your crimes when Malaya is British again."

Yoshimura rushed at Sybil, knocked her down, and kicked her face, again and again, fracturing her jaw.

Dawn was released. Sybil was not. Her interrogations and beatings continued. During one of these sessions, Yoshimura suddenly picked up a heavy wooden bar and beat Sybil across the back with it. One of the blows landed directly on her spine. She fell to the ground and had to be dragged back to her cell. She couldn't walk.

When her trial came, she was sentenced to life in prison.

On August 16, 1945, a British plane dropped some leaflets in the prison courtyard. They read, "The Japanese capitulated on the 15th August, 1945. Until the arrival of the British military authorities, the Malayan People's Anti-Japanese Army will take charge."

After the war, Sybil was flown to England, where she received free medical treatment, including 30 operations, designed to heal the damage caused by Yoshimura's beatings. During this time, she wrote her memoirs and was awarded with the George Medal for courage.

Yoshimura was brought to trial for war crimes on February 10, 1946; Sybil was not the only Malayan civilian he had tortured. In England and too ill to attend the trial, she provided pages of written testimony. Yoshimura was sentenced to death and executed on May 24, 1946.

Although Sybil eventually regained her ability to walk, one day her jaw fracture became infected, quickly leading to septicemia, a fatal blood poisoning.

She died on June 12, 1948.

In 2010, a television miniseries based on her life—*Apa Dosaku: The Sybil Kathigasu Story*—was broadcast in her home country.

LEARN MORE

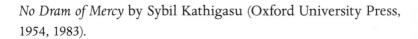

No Dram of Mercy by Sybil Kathigasu (Oxford University Press, 1954, 1983).

Faces of Courage: A Revealing Historical Appreciation of Colonial Malaya's Legendary Kathigasu Family by Sybil Kathigasu, Chin Peng, Norma Miraflor, and Ian Ward (Media Masters, 2006).

ELIZABETH CHOY

"Justice Will Triumph"

ELIZABETH CHOY, BORN Yong Su-Moi in 1910, was never terribly interested in Chinese politics. Her family was part of a Chinese ethnic group called Hakka (literally, "guests"). They had a distinct dialect but no territory of their own. And so, in the late 19th century, Elizabeth's grandparents were very willing to move to the wilds of North Borneo at the invitation of the British, who wanted the land settled by hardworking immigrants.

Elizabeth's Borneo education did little to increase her interest in politics. The missionary boarding school she attended put more emphasis on Christian principles than on politics or current events. When Elizabeth moved to Singapore in 1929 to further her education, one of the few political opinions she held—in common with the large Chinese population of Singapore—was an unshakable faith in the might of the British Empire. Surely Japan would never dare attack British-controlled Malaya or the mighty British fortress at Singapore, which was protected by

Elizabeth Choy. *Ministry of Information and the Arts Collection, Courtesy of National Archives of Singapore*

battleships, enormous guns pointing out toward the sea, and approximately 85,000 Allied soldiers: British, Australian, Indian, and Malayan.

When the Japanese dared to do the unthinkable, bombing Singapore on December 8, 1941, Elizabeth—now a newlywed—could at first hardly believe the reports. But when she encountered the many civilian casualties in the hospital where she volunteered as a nurse, there was no longer any room for doubt.

While on night duty, Elizabeth heard the pounding of shells coming from Malaya. She met a young couple who had seen Japanese soldiers in Malaya, just across the Straits of Johor from Singapore. The Japanese were obviously making their way through the Malayan jungle terrain the British had considered impassable.

Driving to and from the hospital, Elizabeth saw the sad results of the Japanese bombing raids. Civilian casualties lined the roads. Every time the warning siren sounded, everyone ran for their bomb shelters. But most Singaporeans hadn't built quality shelters; one family Elizabeth knew was directly hit while inside their flimsy shelter. The entire family was killed instantly.

Japanese planes also began flying low and targeting civilians. Elizabeth took her family—her siblings, her husband, and her father—to several different locations, hoping each one would be safer than the last. Once, while moving from one place to another, they found themselves high on a hill. They turned and looked down at the rest of the city. It was in flames.

On February 15, 1942, the Allied armies in Singapore were surrounded and their water supply cut off. Concerned about more loss of civilian life, they surrendered to the Japanese. While British prime minister Winston Churchill called Singapore's fall "the worst disaster and the largest capitulation in British history," Japanese emperor Michinomiya Hirohito praised the conquest, claiming it showed "the importance of advance planning."

Elizabeth and her family watched the victors march through the city. "We felt as if that was the end of the world," she said later. "It was terrible."

All Singaporeans were immediately ordered into internment camps for questioning. The women in Elizabeth's family were released quickly. The men were detained longer. Elizabeth's younger brother never returned.

While their men were imprisoned, the women of Elizabeth's family returned home to find the back wall of the kitchen destroyed by shelling. The house had been looted. Elizabeth's wedding gifts were gone.

The women tried to clean and organize as best they could. One day while they were doing this, several Japanese soldiers

★★

THE SOOK CHING MASSACRE

The Sook Ching (literally, "purge through cleansing") massacre was a mass murder of Singapore residents who the Kempeitai considered "undesirable" for one of the following reasons: they were Chinese or were suspected of being either pro-Chinese, Communist, or anti-Japanese. After being questioned and found guilty, the victims were taken to one of Singapore's beaches and murdered. Whereas Japanese historians claim that the total victims of the Sook Ching Massacre numbered less than 5,000, those from Singapore claim the number was much higher.

★★

walked right in. One of them went upstairs and entered the bedroom of Elizabeth's very pregnant sister-in-law. He locked the door. The sister-in-law began to scream, "Save my child! Save my child!"

Elizabeth decided to challenge the intruder. She knocked on the door and cried, "Open! Open! Open!" The soldier quickly opened the door and fled. The other soldiers also left the house, and no one was harmed.

This incident made the women fear sleeping in a house with such easy access. So they slept next door in a garage. All night long, they could hear the Japanese soldiers wandering through the area.

One day, after her father and husband were released, Elizabeth and her husband were approached by the medical staff of a hospital the Japanese had renamed Miyako. It was located in an area without shops or restaurants. The doctors and nurses asked the Choys if they would be willing to open a canteen, commonly called a tuck shop, at the hospital so that the staff could purchase snacks and coffee. They agreed.

Every civilian of British citizenship had by now been arrested and locked up in the Changi prison. Elizabeth was sad to see this: she had many British friends. So she was happy for the opportunity to see them occasionally at the tuck shop; the Japanese allowed sick Changi prisoners to be treated at Miyako. As there was no contact between the prisoners and those on the outside, the Choys agreed to become their link. They first relayed verbal messages, then written notes. Soon the notes were accompanied by packages of food and other items.

Then, on September 14, 1943, seven Japanese ships in the Singapore harbor were blown up. It was the work of a special forces team—Australians and British based in Australia—who had disguised themselves as Indonesian fishermen to do the job.

The Kempeitai mistakenly suspected that this successful sab-otage—code-named Operation Jaywick by the special forces—was somehow connected to the British prisoners in the Changi prison. They made a thorough search and discovered multiple radio sets hidden carefully under prison chairs. The British pris-oners had not only been physically hungry but were also starved for news outside of Japanese-controlled propaganda.

Fifty-seven civilians were taken into Kempeitai custody, interrogated, and brutally tortured. Fifteen were tortured to death. These arrests and interrogations would forever be remembered in Singapore as the Double Tenth Incident, so named because they began on October 10, an important date in the founding of China's Republic.

Where had the prisoners obtained their radio sets? The Kem-peitai were determined to find out. During one particularly brutal interrogation, one of the internees who had been found with a radio admitted he had obtained its parts from the Choys. While passing notes and food, Elizabeth and her husband had also passed radio parts. They rarely knew exactly what was in each package. And they never asked.

On the following day, a car stopped outside the tuck shop. A Kempeitai officer asked Elizabeth's husband, Khun Heng, if he would get into the car: he wasn't familiar with the area, the officer said, and needed help with directions.

Khun Heng agreed to help. He didn't return.

Alarmed, Elizabeth traveled to Kempeitai headquarters with a blanket and extra clothing, pleading with the officers to give the items to her husband.

The officers told Elizabeth they didn't know where he was.

But three weeks later, some Kempeitai officers unexpectedly visited the tuck shop and offered to take Elizabeth to see Khun Heng. When she arrived at the prison, they took her possessions:

her purse, her jewelry, everything except the blanket and clothing she had brought for her husband.

They ushered her into a tiny cell, measuring 10 by 12 feet, so crowded with prisoners—most of them Chinese—there was no room to sit down. Everyone was kneeling or squatting on the floor. It was absolutely silent. No one was allowed to speak. Bugs crawled across the filthy floor. The only piece of furniture was the toilet.

Almost every day, Elizabeth was taken out of the cell, interrogated, beaten, and brutally tortured.

The Kempeitai wanted her to admit she was anti-Japanese and pro-British. She always denied it. "I'm just wanting to help those in need, never mind what race," she would say. "If you should be in the same position, you are my friend, I would help you also." She admitted that she and Khun Heng may have given prisoners radio parts, because they never opened the parcels to check their contents.

Between beatings, the Kempeitai questioned Elizabeth about other things: the seven Japanese ships sunk in the harbor, Australians, money. They asked if she knew this person or that person, claiming each one had already confessed to Elizabeth's role in the sabotage. She denied all knowledge of these accusations. But each day, she was threatened with death if she didn't confess.

"I've told you the truth," she would reply. "I cannot tell you any more."

"Then we are going to execute you."

"All right," she would reply. "If I have to die for telling the truth I will die because truth is very important. I would not tell a lie to save my life."

When the death threat didn't work, they tied her up and tortured her with electric shocks. They brought Khun Heng in to witness her screams.

"Now," they said to the couple, "confess. If not, we'll execute both of you."

As Elizabeth had nothing to confess, the torture continued.

She later claimed the worst agony was the inactivity between interrogations, "being forced to kneel in the cell from morning till night." At night, a guard would come by and say, "Alright, sleep," and they would then lie down next to each other "like sardines," with a bright light shining all night long.

Aside from being in constant painful discomfort, Elizabeth would often worry about her and her family's safety. She tried to combat this through prayer: "I knew nobody on earth could help. I knew there was only one, that is, God."

She also tried to encourage the people around her as much as possible. When the guard wasn't looking, some of the prisoners would communicate with sign language, forming letters with their hands. "If you have not done wrong you will be all right," she would signal to them. "You must believe in that. Justice will triumph."

But she wanted to do more. The stench in the filthy prison made it difficult to breathe. So one day Elizabeth asked the sentry if she could have cleaning tools. While cleaning and passing the other cells, she attempted to silently encourage her fellow prisoners.

When she was rewarded for her work with extra food, she shared it with the thinnest, sickest-looking prisoners in her cell. "It was a joy to do something," she would say later of this gift. "It was a joy."

Although she was not tortured every day, someone in the prison always was. She and the other prisoners could hear their agonizing screams. She would silently pray for each victim, that they would be able to endure it and return. They didn't always.

Elizabeth had endured—up to a point. But after nine months of imprisonment, torture, and starvation rations, she completely lost her appetite. She was on the verge of starving to death.

By this time, the Kempeitai realized she had been telling the truth all along. They called her in one day and told her the results of their investigations: everyone they asked had told them Elizabeth was a humanitarian, someone who was "very kind, very ready to help people." They sent word to her family, requesting extra food be sent in for her.

About a month later, on May 26, 1944, Elizabeth was released. She had been in prison for 193 days. Always quite slim, she had lost half of her original body weight.

She returned to a world paralyzed with fright. Most people in Singapore stayed inside as much as possible. Old friends avoided Elizabeth; since her husband was still in prison, many suspected that she might yet be under surveillance. She was lonely and fearful. But because she had to make a living, she kept busy working as a cashier in a different canteen.

When the Japanese were defeated, Khun Heng was released from prison. Eventually, the British government learned of Elizabeth's arrest—plus her steady behavior under imprisonment and torture. They had already arrested 21 Kempeitai officers involved with the Double Tenth Incident's torture and killing of civilians. They asked Elizabeth which officers she would like to recommend for execution.

She refused to name one. "War is war," she said. "It's not the people who are wicked. War is a wicked thing. The only thing we can do is hope and pray that there would be no more war. If you're an officer you have to do your duty for the country. You have to be brutal and be ruthless as you can."

She traveled to England to regain her health. There she was honored in many ways: she was nominated to represent

Singapore at the coronation of Elizabeth II; she was given a private audience with the Queen Mother; she attended the Victory Buckingham Palace garden party; she was awarded the Order of the British Empire; and she was asked by the British Foreign Office to speak in the United States and Canada. She went, mentioning humorously that she was probably "the first wild woman from Borneo to go to that part of the world to do a lecture tour."

All these events contrasted so starkly with her imprisonment, she felt she had "gone down to the greatest depths of hell and also reached the highest heaven."

In 1951, Elizabeth entered politics, becoming Singapore's first woman in the Legislative Council. She then became an educator and taught in a series of schools for a total of 40 years.

As time passed, she developed a personal philosophy from her horrible prison experiences: "I never expected to come out alive from that Japanese cell. So I've learnt that happiness comes only from within. You do good to others, it will come back to you."

And if Elizabeth's ordeal at the hands of the Kempeitai didn't inspire a lasting hatred for the Japanese, it did cause her to hate one thing for the rest of her life. "There's nothing," she would always say, "so terrible as war."

Elizabeth died on September 14, 2006, at the age of 95.

LEARN MORE

"Elizabeth Choy," *Singapore Infopedia*, http://eresources.nlb.gov
.sg/infopedia/articles/SIP_816_2005-01-25.html?utm_expid
=85360850-6.qNOOYF40RhKK6gXsQEaAJA.0&utm_referrer
=http%3A%2F%2Fsearch.xfinity.com%2F%3Fcon%3Dbeta
search%26cat%3Dweb%26q%3Delizabeth%2Bchoy%2B.

Elizabeth Choy interviews, National Archives of Singapore,
www.nas.gov.sg/archivesonline/oral_history_interviews
/search-result?search-type=advanced&accessionNo=000597.

Elizabeth Choy: More than a War Heroine by Zhou Mei (Landmark
Books, 1995).

VIVIAN BULLWINKEL

Sole Survivor

AUSTRALIAN ARMY NURSE Vivian Bullwinkel walked through the hospital ward for the last time. She fought back tears as she looked at the faces of the wounded men. It was February 12, 1942, and Singapore was falling to the Japanese. She and the other nurses—referred to as nursing sisters—were under orders to evacuate. But none of their patients were complaining. In fact, they were relieved that these nurses, their fellow Australians, would now be safe from the Japanese. The enemy had been attacking Singapore from the air since December 8 and from the ground since February 8, when they had crossed the Straits of Johor from Malaya into Singapore.

Sixty-five Australian nurses boarded a tugboat in the harbor and headed for a large ship named *Vyner Brooke*, which was also carrying numerous civilians. Vivian looked back at the shore. Darkness was falling, but the besieged city was lit up in flames. Billowing black smoke could be seen for miles back.

Vivian Bullwinkel, 1941, Puckapunyal Army Camp, Victoria, Australia, before she left for Singapore. *National Library of Australia,* © *Bruce Howard*

Vivian looked at the other nurses. Their eyes were filled with tears. Vivian was certain they all had the same thing on their minds: the doomed men they had left behind.

Were the nurses doomed as well? They had escaped the main area of fighting, but the air and seas around Singapore were now controlled by the Japanese. Would they make it to Australia?

Not if the Japanese could help it. The next day, the deck of the *Vyner Brooke* was covered with dozing nurses and civilian women and children. They were passing near the islands of the Dutch East Indies. Vivian heard a droning off in the distance. She saw a black speck on the horizon.

The speck came nearer. It was a plane. It was flying low and heading straight for the ship.

"Take cover!" shouted the captain. The Japanese plane fired into the water before turning around and flying back. No one was seriously hurt.

But the enemy had seen them. The captain tried to move out of the area, but on the following day, several additional Japanese planes attacked the *Vyner Brooke*. The first bombs exploded only feet from the ship. Sailors scrambled to get the anti-aircraft guns in place. The next bombs hit the ship. Explosions rocked the deck and tipped it dangerously. Women and children were screaming. Most of them jumped overboard or into lifeboats hastily lowered into the churning water.

Not content with destroying the ship, the Japanese planes returned and took aim at the survivors: the men, women, and children who were still struggling to abandon ship or those already in the water whose buoyant lifejackets kept them from diving underwater.

As the ship sank, it rolled over and crushed a lifeboat packed with women and children. Vivian saw the bodies of small children, too tiny for lifejackets, floating amid the debris before they disappeared beneath the surface. Life-jacketed corpses floated away.

The survivors, including Vivian, paddled and kicked as best they could toward the visible shore, fighting the current that threatened to drag them far out to sea.

After seven exhausting hours, Vivian finally felt something solid under her feet. She walked ashore and collapsed on Radji Beach, of Banka Island in the Dutch East Indies.

There, Vivian was reunited with some of the people from the *Vyner Brooke*, including 21 of her fellow Australian nurses, a few members of the ship's crew, civilian passengers, and a large group of British servicemen whose ship had also been sunk.

A local man told them Banka Island was under the control of the Japanese. The military personnel had heard rumors that the Japanese didn't take military prisoners. But since there were women and children with them, perhaps the group's best chance of survival would be surrender.

The next morning, First Officer Bill Sedgman of the *Vyner Brooke* decided to contact the nearest Japanese troops. His plan was to then lead the Japanese back to the beach for an official surrender. Most of the civilians went with them. The nurses stayed at the beach to care for the wounded.

As the group walked away, Vivian's thoughts became very dark. She sensed something terrible was about to happen. But instead of dwelling on her gloomy forebodings, she fetched fresh water for everyone from a stream.

A few hours later, the sailors returned to the beach without the civilians but accompanied by a large group of Japanese soldiers. "These are the people I told you about," said Sedgman to the Japanese officer in charge. "They want to become your prisoners of war."

Vivian studied the face of the Japanese commander. It was emotionless. He said something to the soldiers. They immediately filled their machine guns and rifles—all with attached bayonets—with ammunition. The soldiers pointed their weapons at the group of people.

Vivian felt nauseous. Sedgman protested. The Japanese officer ignored him. Using their bayonets, the soldiers separated the British servicemen from the Australian nurses. The men were marched out of sight. The Japanese officer stayed with the nurses. A few moments later, Vivian heard gunfire. Then silence.

The Japanese soldiers came back chatting and laughing, each of them cleaning his bayonet with a cloth. The British servicemen were not with them.

"Bully," one nurse said, addressing Vivian, "They've murdered them all!"

Vivian was silent.

"It's true then, they aren't taking prisoners," said another nurse.

The Japanese officer said something to his soldiers. They surrounded the 22 Australian nurses. They prodded the nurses with their bayonets until the women had formed a line into the water. Two wounded nurses had to be half carried there by their companions.

It seemed impossible to Vivian that a mass slaughter was about to occur in this beautiful setting. She kept asking herself why. And what right did the Japanese have to kill them?

But she said nothing aloud. None of the nurses did. Except for the sound of the water hitting their thighs, the beach was silent. Vivian, sad to think her mother would never learn what happened to her, suddenly felt peaceful when she realized she would soon see her deceased father. She wanted to communicate her new emotion to the other nurses. She turned and smiled at them. They returned her smile "in a strange and beautiful way."

They had obviously found their own ways to cope during these last terrible moments.

Then Vivian heard the whispered voice of their matron, Irene Drummond, "Chin up girls, I'm proud of you and I love you all."

The quiet was abruptly shattered by the roar of guns. The ammunition churned the clear water into white foam. Then the water turned dark red. Bullets ripped into the bodies of the nurses, who either crumpled or were flung forward. Vivian stood still and waited for death.

She felt an enormous blow hit her lower back. She fell below the surface of the water. "So this is what it is like to get shot and die," she thought. Everything went black.

Then she woke up. "I'm not dead," was her first, obvious thought. She was floating on the water. She listened intently. She heard nothing but the sound of birds and the wind rustling through the palm trees.

She drifted in and out of consciousness. Then, wide awake, she found herself on the beach. It was deserted. The entire bay was deserted. She was alone.

Had the Japanese removed the bodies? If so, why hadn't they taken hers? She realized the bodies of her friends must have had been caught in a rip tide and carried out to sea. For some reason Vivian could not quite understand, hers had stayed in the bay.

She checked her wound and felt where the bullet had entered the back of her left hip and exited through the front of her left side. Because she was hardly bleeding, Vivian assumed the bullet had missed her vital organs.

She limped over to some dense foliage just off the beach and fell asleep. When she woke up, she heard a metallic click. She saw the flash of a bayonet. She heard the chatter of Japanese voices.

Concealed by the foliage, she watched a group of Japanese soldiers file past. She recognized some of them: these were the same men who had murdered her friends and tried to murder her. Her heart was pounding. She was shaking. But the soldiers didn't notice her and passed by.

Several hours later, when she felt it was safe enough to come out of hiding, Vivian rushed to the freshwater stream and began to drink.

"Where have you been, nurse?" Vivian whipped around to see who had spoken. It was a young man in a British army uniform.

His name was Private Kinsley. He had been one of the wounded on the beach and had witnessed the nurse massacre. After killing the nurses, the Japanese returned to the wounded and bayoneted them. Kinsley survived, despite being stabbed twice.

Vivian inspected his wounds. They were already badly infected. He would not survive unless immediately hospitalized. Since this was impossible, Vivian determined to stay with him till he died.

Vivian and Kinsley were, by this time, ravenously hungry. Vivian decided to ask some locals for food. After walking along a rugged trail in bare feet for several painful miles, she entered the outskirts of a village where she saw women cooking in large pots. She asked the head of the village if they would provide food for her and Kinsley on a regular basis.

He refused and instead suggested they turn themselves in. Desperate, she turned to the cooking women and asked, "Please, just a little food."

They looked at her but said nothing.

In despair, Vivian turned to go. She and Kinsley would both starve to death.

Then she noticed movement in the jungle along the path. Two local women emerged. Smiling, they placed two bundles of food on the ground, then disappeared as quickly as they had come. Several days later, Vivian returned to the same spot and the same smiling women again gave her food.

Kinsley and Vivian survived on this food for 11 days. But how long would these women provide for them? Kinsley was clearly not going to survive without hospitalization. And Vivian suddenly realized she didn't want to die alone.

She decided they should take a chance and surrender to the Japanese at Muntok headquarters, a few miles away. Kinsley immediately agreed, saying "If it comes to the worst I hope the Japs do a better job of it this time."

Before leaving, Vivian washed their uniforms as best she could; she didn't want the Japanese to realize she and Kinsley had survived the massacre. Then they began the long, exhausting trip to Muntok, Kinsley dividing his weight between Vivian and a cane.

When they reached the headquarters, they had a few moments to say good-bye.

"I want you to know that I admire you very much," Vivian whispered to Kinsley, "and I feel a great pride in having had you as a companion."

"I would never have made it thus far," Kinsley replied, "if it hadn't been for you, Sister. I used to look at you and wonder, what with everything that happened to you, where you got your strength from to go on. You set the example Sister, you made me determined to be like you."

A car pulled up to take Kinsley away. As Vivian sadly watched him go, a group of captured Allied servicemen walked by. "All these fine young men," Vivian thought, "the pride of their countries, overwhelmed and defeated in such a short space in time, being marched off to a prison camp." Vivian didn't realize it then, but most of the POWs who survived the prison camp would wind up as slave laborers on the Burma Railway, one of the most horrific war crimes of the Pacific Theater.

When she was taken to a women's internment camp, Vivian was overjoyed to see some Australian nursing sisters from the *Vyner Brooke* who had drifted to a different Banka Island beach. They surrounded her excitedly. Where had she been, they asked, and where were the others?

★★★

THE BURMA RAILWAY

The construction of the 257-mile Burma Railway—also known as the Death Railway—was overseen by the Japanese military, who wanted a transportation line from Thailand, which they controlled, to Burma, where they were battling the British. The reason no one had yet built a railway through this remote, mountainous jungle area—although the British had considered it decades earlier—was because the heat, humidity, and jungle diseases would cause nearly impossible working conditions. This didn't stop the Japanese, especially when the Allied surrender at Singapore gave them an entire army of slave labor. Fed starvation rations and given hand tools for their work, the men—60,000 Allied POWs and 200,000 Asian civilians—forced to build the Burma Railway were worked, literally, to death: by October 1943, when the railway was completed, approximately 100,000 of its forced laborers had died.

★★★

Vivian's smile faded. She was silent. Finally, she said, "They're all dead."

She told them the tale. They agreed to not speak of it in the camp again; the massacre was clearly a war crime. If the Japanese discovered a surviving witness, Vivian would certainly be killed.

A few days later, she was called to the men's camp hospital. Someone had been asking for her. It was Kinsley. He was near death.

"Sister," Kinsley whispered when he saw Vivian.

"Yes, Kinsley, it's me."

"Thank you . . . for everything Sister."

He tried to squeeze her hand. "You . . . had better . . . go now." He closed his eyes.

Vivian remembered something she'd learned in nursing school, a quote from Florence Nightingale: "No soldier should die alone upon a foreign soil."

"I'll stay with you a little while longer, Kinsley."

Vivian held his hand as he slipped away. Twenty minutes later, he was dead.

During the next three years, Vivian, the nurses, and Dutch and English women and children held captive with them attempted to survive in a series of internment camps where the quality of life, along with the quantity of food and medicine, deteriorated steadily. Many prisoners died of starvation or jungle illnesses. But the survivors did whatever they could to keep their spirits alive in spite of their weakened health.

One of the more creative means of boosting morale in any of the Far East women's camps was something called the vocal orchestra (chapter 13). Created by British civilians Margaret Dryburgh and Norah Chambers, and including some of Vivian's fellow Australian nursing sisters, the vocal orchestra became a powerful symbol of survival to most of the women in the camp. Vivian was a faithful member of the audience whenever the orchestra performed.

After the war, in October 1946, Vivian traveled to Tokyo to give testimony of the Banka Island massacre. In a clear, strong voice, she recounted the entire story. When she finished and stood up to leave the witness box, she was trembling.

Before she returned to Australia, she was told that Captain Maru Orita, the officer who had ordered the massacre, committed suicide in his cell.

Vivian retired from the army in 1947 and became the director of nursing at a civilian hospital in Melbourne. She raised funds for a memorial to her colleagues who had died on Banka Island, before returning there in 1992 in order to unveil a shrine in their honor.

She died in 2000 at the age of 84.

LEARN MORE

Bullwinkel: The True Story of Vivian Bullwinkel, a Young Army Nursing Sister, Who Was the Sole Survivor of a World War Two Massacre by the Japanese by Norman G. Manners (Hesperian, 1999).

On Radji Beach by Ian W. Shaw (MacMillan Australia, 2010).

Surviving Tenko: The Story of Margot Turner by Penny Starns (History Press, 2010). Turner's shipwreck experiences were similar to Vivian Bullwinkel's, and they wound up in the same internment camp.

HELEN COLIJN

Rising Above

THE JAPANESE GUARD held up two fingers. Only two graves. A few days earlier it had been eight.

Helen Colijn, a Dutch teenager, along with three other prisoners, had volunteered for grave duty. Sometimes digging graves didn't seem as depressing as living in the filthy internment camp with all of the starving, sick, and dying women.

Helen's view of death had changed drastically during her imprisonment. It was no longer a shock, and barely a sorrow. It occurred nearly every day. Few of the surviving prisoners still had the energy to grieve.

But Helen could do something to help: she could dig. The guards wouldn't do it, so it was up to the prisoners. She wished the guards would at least give them better digging tools. The older women had repeatedly requested actual spades, but they were always ignored. The prisoners were given as little as possible of everything: food, medicine, clothing, blankets. Or effective tools with which to dig graves.

At least the ground wasn't hard today; it had just rained. Still, the simple mattock Helen was using felt heavy. She had to pause from time to time because her heart began to race. Sometimes she experienced a short blackout. She was glad the guard was dozing under a tree; otherwise he would have certainly shouted, *Lekas, lekas!* (Quickly, quickly!)

Exhausted and weak as she was, Helen and the other teenager digging with her dug so deeply that eventually one of them had to climb inside the grave to continue.

As Helen dug from inside, she began to imagine her own funeral. Would her coffin be long enough? She was six feet tall. The Japanese provided only flimsy, short coffins; it was always difficult for the women to bury their too tall friends. Helen would probably not be buried in her "liberation" dress, the outfit she was saving for the day she hoped to be rescued by the victorious Allies. Her two sisters, Antoinette and Alette, would be able to use it.

Who would conduct her funeral? How would they write her name on the cross? Would it be Helen Colijn or Helen C. Colijn?

She quickly stopped herself from thinking this way. If she still had enough strength to dig a grave, she certainly wouldn't be needing one soon. Though emaciated, Helen was actually healthy compared to some of the other prisoners, many of whom were dying not only from the lack of food and medicine but because they had lost the will to live.

Helen had everything to live for: her sisters were with her, and their father, Anton Colijn, was surely nearby in a men's camp. Their mother, Zus, had been imprisoned by the Japanese elsewhere. She hadn't evacuated with her family from their home on the island of Tarakan, part of the Dutch East Indies.

The Colijn sisters, 1939 in the Dutch East Indies. Left to right: Antoinette, Helen, Alette. Song of Survival *by Helen Colijn (White Cloud Press, 1995), used by permission of the publisher*

Zus insisted her Red Cross nurse work was crucial and would prevent her arrest. It hadn't.

Her father, on the other hand, knew that because he was a reserve member of the Dutch army, he would certainly be imprisoned. Long before the Japanese landed on Tarakan, he realized their tiny, oil-rich island would not be overlooked by the Japanese; the Japanese needed oil because the Allied nations had stopped giving it to them.

When the Japanese first attacked the Dutch East Indies, the Colijn girls did whatever they could to support the war effort. But those efforts were brief; the Dutch soon capitulated to the Japanese.

Anton Colijn could have escaped on a plane carrying other military personnel, but his daughters would not have been able to accompany him. So they all fled on an Australian-bound ship, which was bombed and destroyed by Japanese planes. Helen and her father became separated from Alette and Antoinette. After spending an entire week in a lifeboat with other ship-wreck survivors, Helen and her father landed on the shores of Tabuan Island. Shortly after being reunited there with Alette and Antoinette, Japanese sentries arrested them all. The Colijn girls were then separated from their father, who was taken to a men's camp.

Helen and her sisters were taken to an internment camp, referred to as a "houses" camp because it consisted of many individual structures. Imprisoned with them were other civilians, Dutch and British women and children, along with a group of Australian Army nurses.

The most difficult part of camp life was *tenko*, the term Japanese prison guards used during the war for roll call. Every day women and children were ordered, *"Keirei!"*—to bow from the waist to the guard who was the local representative of the Japanese emperor. Any gesture that could possibly be interpreted as a slight to Emperor Hirohito—a smirk, a comment, not bowing low enough—could result in a vicious slap or kick. Sometimes the women were made to stand in the hot sun for hours if one of them didn't get it quite right.

There were also rules for those outside the camp. An elderly Chinese man who lived nearby was caught trying to sell the starving women some duck eggs. The Japanese guards hauled him into the camp, tied him to a pole, then wrapped a rope around his neck and hands in a way that would strangle him if he tried to lower his arms.

It took three days for him to die. During that time, everyone in the camp, including small children, had to walk past the tortured man on their way to *tenko*. A British woman who tried to sneak him a glass of water was discovered by a guard and savagely beaten, almost to death.

But the guards did allow the prisoners to conduct their own educational group activities. Some held classes for the children, while others shared their languages or other skills with adults. There was also a communal library. The women chafed at being imprisoned without contact with the outside world and having their food rations so limited, but they also had some time to enjoy themselves.

That all changed early in 1943 when they were moved into a hastily constructed barracks camp. Everyone had only a tiny area of individual living space. The latrines were public. Bathing was public. Everyone had to take part in communal jobs for the entire camp, not just the people in their "house." This meant more work and less energy for anything educational.

Near the end of the year, Antoinette complained to Helen, "If this goes on for long, we'll be reduced to a grey mass of regulated, automated prisoners."

Two English prisoners decided to create something that would make a difference. One of them was Margaret Dryburgh, a musically gifted missionary who often led Sunday services for the prisoners and who had already written a very moving song for the prisoners called "The Captives Hymn." She and Norah Chambers, a trained musician, formed a choir composed of Dutch, English, and Australian singers. They met at night in the camp kitchen to rehearse. Their first concert was rumored to be something very special, but no one outside of the choir was given any details.

Alette and Antoinette were both in the choir. A date was set for the first concert. The day before, Antoinette asked Helen to walk through each barrack to formally announce it.

★★★

EXCERPTS FROM "THE CAPTIVES HYMN" BY MARGARET DRYBURGH

Father, in captivity
We would lift our prayer to thee . . .
Give us patience to endure
Keep our hearts serene and pure,
Grant us courage, charity,
Greater faith, humility,
Readiness to own Thy Will,
Be we free or captive still . . .

May the day of freedom dawn
Peace and justice be reborn,
Grant that nations loving Thee
O'er the world may brothers be,
Cleansed by suffering, know rebirth,
See Thy Kingdom come on earth.

★★★

Helen was shy. "Everyone knows already there will be a concert," she protested.

"But if you take the trouble to *announce* it, it will add importance," Antoinette insisted. "Get yourself a tin and a stick and cry out the news, like an old-fashioned town crier."

On the day of the concert, Alette and Antoinette left their section of the barracks, calling behind them to Helen, "Enjoy our surprise."

Helen put on her liberation dress. An unpleasant woman who the Colijn girls referred to as Mrs. Sergeant Major saw her and said, "You must be going to that concert. It's absurd to waste precious energy singing. The singers should be using their energy for just staying alive!"

"But the singers say they generate energy by singing," Helen answered.

"Could be. But we all know the Japanese don't want us to gather in crowds. To have a whole mass of us in the compound, listening to I don't care what, is inviting disaster. The guard will lose his temper and we'll all have to stand in the sun again. *I* am *not* going."

As Helen walked to join the concert's audience, she was glad she had taken the trouble to formally announce it. The gathered crowd was clearly excited: children nicely groomed by their mothers; adults, like Helen, wearing their liberation dresses; and a group of Australian nurses all wearing the same shade of lipstick.

Then Helen saw the word *ORCHESTRA* scratched in large letters in the dirt. Orchestra? She knew there were no real instruments in camp. Had she generated excitement for a performance played on crude homemade instruments?

They would all soon find out. A few minutes later, 30 women, each holding a piece of paper in one hand and a stool in the other, filed out of the main kitchen to face the audience. Children sat in front, while many of the adults, including Helen, stood.

Then Margaret Dryburgh spoke. "This evening," she said, "we are asking you to listen to something quite new, we are sure: a choir of women's voices trying to reproduce some of the well-known music usually given by an orchestra or a pianist." The singers, she said, would sit on their stools just like orchestra performers, in order to conserve their energy.

Then she took her place among the singers. Norah Chambers stood in front of the performers. She raised her hands. The choir began to sing, in four-part harmony, Dvorak's "Largo" from the New World Symphony.

"The music soared in its first rich and full crescendo," Helen wrote later. "I felt a shiver go down my back. I thought I had never heard anything so beautiful before. The music didn't sound precisely like an orchestra either, although it was close. . . . The music sounded ethereal, totally unreal in our sordid surroundings."

"Huu, huu." Helen heard a new sound, "the ugly raw voice of an angry guard," coming up behind her. Surely Norah could hear it too. But she didn't stop directing the music.

"Huu, huu." The angry guard, his bayonet fixed on his rifle, passed through the standing audience. Soon Helen could only see the tip of his bayonet.

The music continued. The angry voice did not. Helen craned her neck: she could no longer see the bayonet. Had the guard put down his weapon? Was he also mesmerized by the beautiful music?

Apparently so. "As the Largo moved toward a great, glorious crescendo," Helen would write later, "the guard remained as still as we" for the rest of the concert.

During the intermission, one of the women serving refreshments offered a tiny homemade rice flour cookie to the guard, who, Helen wrote later, "looked oddly alone in a sea of captive women." He accepted the cookie with thanks. Helen wondered if the music had brought back memories or if it was the first time he had heard classical European music. She thought perhaps he "may have been as lonely as we were, caught up in the idiocies of war."

The orchestra presented more concerts. One of them was attended by three Japanese officers, each respectfully wearing a formal uniform and polished boots. Helen attended every concert. "Each time we heard the music," she wrote later, "we marveled again at the beautiful and often familiar melodies, at the purity of sound, at this miracle that was happening to us amid the cockroaches, the rats, the bedbugs, and the stink of the latrines. The music renewed our sense of human dignity. We had to live under bestial conditions but, by Jove, we could rise above them!"

But by the time Helen began volunteering to dig graves on the island of Bangka, the location of the third camp, the vocal orchestra was no more. Too many of its members had died, and the remaining singers were too starved to continue.

On April 21, 1945, Margaret Dryburgh died shortly after the prisoners were moved to a fourth camp. Although most camp funerals were attended only by those who carried the coffin and perhaps a representative of that person's nation, Margaret's funeral was attended by many prisoners, including all the surviving members of the vocal orchestra strong enough to walk up the hill to the cemetery.

Four months later, on August 24, 1945, the prisoners who were not bedridden were summoned to a spot outside the guardhouse. The camp commander told them the war was over. He didn't tell them who had won.

The following day, the women began to receive items they'd previously been told were unavailable: food, medicine, blankets, bandages, mosquito nets, towels. Many weak prisoners continued to die, and all of them had to carry on in the squalor of the camp. But they were no longer starving. And they knew help was on the way.

On September 7, 1945, Dutch paratroopers entered the camp. They said "they had never seen such awful conditions [in the camps they'd been liberating] and were amazed that anyone could live like this."

Australian soldiers, who entered the camp shortly after-ward, brought the women news and rumors. Two Japanese cities, they said, had been completely destroyed by one bomb each. Not only had these bombs ended the war, the soldiers said, but they may have saved the women's lives: their camp had been scheduled for annihilation on August 31, the birthday of Dutch Queen Wilhelmina.

Helen was now so weak she could not walk far. While waiting for the promised transport, she moved her hospital cot outside during the day so that she could watch the planes drop food into the camp. When she saw the red, white, and blue of the Dutch flag on these planes, instead of the Japanese rising sun emblem, she finally allowed herself to believe the war was over.

When she was released from the camp and hospitalized in Singapore, six-foot-tall Helen weighed only 90 pounds.

Helen's father did not survive the war. Her mother did. The Colijn women moved to the United States, where they rarely discussed the war.

But in 1980, Antoinette rediscovered her 68-page booklet of vocal orchestra scores. The tiny, carefully penciled notes were beginning to fade. She decided to donate it to Stanford University. This started a series of events that brought international attention to the vocal orchestra. A California choir learned the music and performed it at a concert whose audience included the surviving members of the vocal orchestra. A documentary film, a feature film, and a CD eventually followed.

While being interviewed for the documentary, Antoinette described how the rehearsals had helped her: "[Norah] never let a false note or a muddled phrasing go by. She made us go back again and again, until we got the music just right. But to sing measure 32 and 33 correctly became very important and took your mind off whether you were hungry, or thirsty, or feeling sick, or just plain down in the dumps."

Betty Jeffrey, an Australian member of the orchestra, said during her interview, "When I sang that vocal orchestra music, I forgot I was in the camp. I felt free."

Helen died in 2006 at the age of 85.

LEARN MORE

Song of Survival: Women Interned by Helen Colijn (White Cloud Press, 1995).

Song of Survival DVD (Janson Media, 2000). This documentary has interviews of the vocal choir.

Paradise Road CD (Sony, 1997). This CD features a women's choir singing music from the vocal orchestra scores.

PART IV

Iwo Jima and Okinawa

JANE KENDEIGH

Navy Flight Nurse

ON FEBRUARY 19, 1945, 20-year-old William Wyckoff was on his way to Iwo Jima. He was one of 40,000 young marines who were the first Americans heading for the small volcanic island. Little could grow there, and only a few Japanese civilians had lived there before their government evicted them, as the Americans approached.

US military strategists were determined to have Iwo Jima in US hands. Since their decisive win at the Battle of Midway in 1942, the United States had been taking Japanese-controlled Pacific islands in one grindingly bloody victory after another. Iwo Jima was closer to the Japanese home islands than any other island currently under US control. And it was only 660 miles south of Tokyo, Japan's capital city, a major target for US air raids.

But this battle wasn't going to be easy. Although Japanese military leaders realized they didn't have the means to repulse

Jane Kendeigh surrounded by US marines, April 7, 1945, minutes after becoming the first navy flight nurse to land on Okinawa. *US Navy Bureau of Medicine and Surgery (BUMED) Library and Archives*

the US invasion, they were still determined to fight for Iwo Jima: unlike the other islands under American control, Iwo Jima was technically Japanese soil. To defend it was to defend their national honor.

So they went to work, well before the approach of the Americans. Below Iwo Jima's ashy surface were hundreds of natural caves. The Japanese commander in charge of the island's defense ordered his men to enlarge and link these caves with tunnels. The caves were then manned by approximately 20,000 Japanese fighting men ordered to defend their positions—to the death.

As young William approached and saw the anti-aircraft fire from the island shooting down the US carrier planes, he knew the Americans were in for a furious fight.

He was right. When he and the other marines scurried up the beach, they were attacked with an endless torrent of ammunition fired from a well-hidden enemy who could obviously see them clearly. Confused and deeply frustrated, the young marines sometimes fired back aimlessly.

The only available shelter was the occasional crater from the US Navy's earlier bombardment. But these craters didn't always provide sufficient protection. After crawling into one, William's shoulder and forehead were grazed by an onslaught of bullets. A marine sharing his crater was shot and killed. By the beginning of March, thousands of young marines were dead or wounded.

One evening, after William's superior officer ordered him to lead his squad in an assault the following morning, William told one of his men he "had a bad feeling" about the next day. The man was surprised; William wasn't usually so negative.

The next day, William led the charge. He heard a shout in Japanese. Then everything went black.

When he regained consciousness, he was lying on his back. His left shoulder was in excruciating pain. It was difficult to hear. It was difficult to see. Even so, he was alarmed by a sudden flash of bright light. He tried to jump up. He couldn't. Then he heard something that surprised him even more than the light: the voice of a woman. "Don't worry," said 22-year-old Jane Kendeigh. "It's only Navy photographers."

Jane Kendeigh had wanted to become a nurse for as long as she could remember. After graduating from nursing school and joining the navy, she was accepted into a training program for something new: flight nursing.

Flight evacuation came about during World War II because of speed—or the lack of it: severely wounded men had a better chance of surviving if transported by air rather than the usual hospital ship. In 1942, American casualties of the Pacific War

Jane Kendeigh attempts to comfort William Wyckoff, Iwo Jima, March 6, 1945. *US Navy Bureau of Medicine and Surgery (BUMED) Library and Archives*

were evacuated via cargo planes, the first ones with no trained medics on board. Pharmacists were added, then flight surgeons.

The US Army was the first branch of the military to open its own flight nursing school. The US Navy followed, and in January 1945, its first graduating class included 24 female navy nurses and 24 male pharmacist mates. Jane was one of the nurses.

During the flight school's two-month training course, Jane and the other trainees learned how high altitudes could damage the bodies of already wounded men.

They were also taught what to do if forced to evacuate over water. To qualify for this part of the course, each trainee had to swim a mile, swim underwater (to escape burning oil if the ship crashed), climb onto a life raft, and jump into water from a distance of ten feet.

Jane's first flight into a combat zone began on March 6, 1945, when her plane took off from the US-controlled island of Guam. Besides Jane and the plane crew, a male pharmacist's mate, Silas Sturtevant, was also on board and would be taking orders from Jane. Accompanying them was Lieutenant Gill DeWitt, a very disappointed navy photographer. He had been assigned to photograph the first navy flight nurse to land on Iwo Jima but had missed the first plane's takeoff by a few minutes. The next best thing, he thought, was photographing the nurse on the second flight.

"There's Iwo," announced the plane's radioman as they approached the island. But it wasn't yet safe to land. The plane had to circle Iwo Jima for an hour and a half while US ships just offshore pounded the island in an attempt to destroy the caves and bunkers sheltering Japanese snipers.

Meanwhile, the plane's passengers could clearly see the front line of fighting: the fire of weapons left a cloud of smoke and dust. The "bursting shells" fired from the many US battleships reminded Lieutenant DeWitt of "firecrackers on the Fourth of July."

Although the plane was high enough to be clear of the US bombardment, it was certainly visible to the Japanese snipers below. Jane knew that Japanese anti-aircraft guns on the island had already shot down US carrier planes. One of those guns might still be in action. But an anti-aircraft gun wouldn't be necessary to take them down; a single bullet hitting the fuel tank would cause the plane to explode.

So Jane and the others were relieved when the plane finally swished past the highest point on the island—Mount Suribachi—and settled in for a landing.

Jane's destination was beside the airstrip: a small sandbagged hospital tent. The roar of guns and artillery was so loud, Jane and Silas could barely hear one another speaking as they hurried inside. There they found doctors and male medics working frantically to save lives in rough conditions. The stretcher-bearers carried wounded men out of the tent and lined them up near the waiting plane. Jane spoke comfortingly to each man, if he was conscious, and checked him as he went aboard.

Meanwhile, Lieutenant DeWitt asked the medics in the tent about the previous plane, the one he'd missed. They told him it was due in very soon; the pilot had lost his way.

This delay meant that Jane Kendeigh had suddenly become front-page news: the first navy flight nurse to land on Iwo Jima, the first navy flight nurse to step onto a World War II Pacific battlefield. Lieutenant DeWitt's photograph of her speaking to William was transmitted to the United States, where it appeared in nearly every newspaper in the nation.

This would not be the last time she would have her photo taken by military photographers. As the first navy flight nurse to land on Okinawa as well as Iwo Jima, Jane remained big news for the rest of the war. Referred to as an Angel of Mercy and Candy Kendeigh (referring to a popular song of the time), she was always gracious to photographers. But she was much more interested in doing her job than having her photo taken, even though she understood that her image was appearing in newspapers all over America. When she was ordered to go on a monthlong war bond tour to raise necessary money from US citizens for the war effort, she followed orders but was "anxious" to return to her real job: landing in battle zones and caring for wounded men in flight.

Did she ever get used to the danger? On that first flight back from Iwo, Silas asked Jane, "Were you frightened by the firing?"

She thought for a moment, remembering how, while on the island, "her knees had quaked and her breath came short." Yes, apparently she had been frightened, but was too excited to realize it. Explaining later how she was able to function in spite of

Jane and pharmacist's mate Silas Sturtevant familiarize themselves with patient information on their way from Iwo Jima to Guam. *US Navy Bureau of Medicine (BUMED) and Surgery Library and Archives*

her fears, she said, "You live on your nerves. It was after I got back to Guam that I got thinking about it. Gee, I really went through that."

She would go through it again and again. The routine on each flight was basically the same. The battle zone medics would explain what each patient would require on the flight. The plane was arranged to hold stretchers strapped to the sides of the plane.

Jane was always very busy on the flight back, keeping constant watch over her patients: checking their vital signs—blood pressure, temperature, etc.—feeding those who needed help, and keeping everyone as comfortable as possible.

Dozens of navy flight nurses treated more than 2,000 men on flights from Iwo Jima in March 1945, and nearly 12,000 from Okinawa the following June; larger planes were gradually used to accommodate more patients per flight. Yet none of these women received any official awards for their efforts. In an article she wrote for a US Navy magazine, Jane explained her take on this oversight: "Perhaps you're wondering about the compensation in this duty—our rewards are wan smiles, a slow nod of appreciation, a gesture, a word—accolades greater, more heart-warming than any medal."

Just talking to the soldiers, putting her hand on theirs, helped soothe them. "It was so unexpected for them to have a girl to talk to," she said later, "they just wanted to hang on to you." Sometimes the weakened men, nauseated by the high altitude, hung on so close, they threw up on her, which greatly embarrassed the men conscious enough to realize what they'd done.

William Wyckoff was one of these men. Although he survived his wounds and even regained his eyesight, he never fully recovered from the embarrassment of having heaved on Jane Kendeigh during his flight from Iwo Jima to Guam. Forty-one

★★

THE PRICE OF AN AIRFIELD

Once Iwo Jima was in US control, it was used as an airfield in support of approximately 2,000 bombing raids until
Okinawa, closer to Japan, replaced it. But those airfields
were seized at an enormous cost. When American flyer
Paul Montgomery first landed on Iwo Jima, he was overwhelmed when he saw the island's graveyard: "I had never
seen 7,000 markers before," he said. "And when I came
to realize that they were just kids like myself and that they
wouldn't be going home . . . it just took something out of me
that I didn't know was there. . . . I became traumatized with
the price that had been paid so I could have a runway to
land on coming back."

★★

years later, at a reunion of Iwo Jima veterans where Jane was the
guest of honor, William thought he finally found his chance to
apologize. Jane, now the wife of a former navy pilot, the mother
of three, and a nurse in a doctor's office, had never forgotten
William either. But when he tried to apologize for the mess he'd
made back in 1945, Jane said to him, "Now just you never mind
about that."

"She hasn't changed a bit," said William.

Jane died in 1987.

LEARN MORE

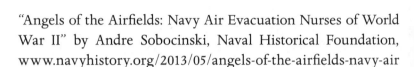

"Angels of the Airfields: Navy Air Evacuation Nurses of World War II" by Andre Sobocinski, Naval Historical Foundation, www.navyhistory.org/2013/05/angels-of-the-airfields-navy-air-evacuation-nurses-ww2/.

Navy Flight Nurses of World War II by Andre Sobocinski, Naval Historical Foundation, www.med.navy.mil/bumed/nmhistory/Pages/showcase/Innovations/FlightNurses/main.aspx. Contains a photograph slide show.

The First Navy Flight Nurse on a Pacific Battlefield: A Picture Story of a Flight to Iwo Jima by Lieutenant Gill DeWitt (Admiral Nimitz Foundation, 1983).

DICKEY CHAPELLE

"As Far Forward as You'll Let Me"

"ARE YOU A WRITER or a photographer?"

Twenty-five-year-old Georgette Louise "Dickey" Chapelle wasn't sure how to answer the question. The only direction her editor at Fawcett Publications had given her when she told him she wanted to report on the women of the Pacific War was, "Just be sure you're first someplace."

She told the navy press liaison officer that she had worked as both a writer *and* a photographer.

"You can't be both," he replied. "On operations, you may use radio facilities if you are a writer, or your camera if you are a photographer. But only one."

Dickey didn't think she'd heard him right. Had he just said "operations"? That word, Dickey was quite certain, implied combat. But the military did not allow women reporters to cover combat. If she broke the rules, she would certainly lose her accreditation—her official permission to report on anything

Dickey Chapelle, 1942, self-portrait. *Wisconsin State Historical Society, Image #64787*

related to the war. Perhaps she could find a way to bend the rules instead of breaking them.

She asked the officer how many accredited women reporters the navy had already sent out. There were a few, he said. And how many accredited female photographers?

"Never heard of one," he answered.

"I'm a photographer, then," said Dickey.

"Very well," he replied. "And just where was it you wanted to go?"

"As far forward as you'll let me."

The female military personnel in the Pacific—the WAVES (Women Accepted for Volunteer Emergency Service) and the WACs (Women's Army Corps)—had gone as far as Honolulu. So that's where Dickey went via plane from California, on February 19, 1945, along with a group of navy flight nurses just out of training.

During this trip, Dickey heard the name Iwo Jima for the first time. The copilot, climbing back to speak to Dickey and the nurses, told them the Americans had just landed there. A few days later, Dickey was standing in front of the teletype machine in Oahu watching the reports come in from Iwo Jima. "There was not one," she wrote later, "that did not tell of fresh disaster. Whole outfits [units of fighting men] were being . . . decimated, destroyed."

Someone in the room said that "the Corps" wouldn't be able to take this much longer.

"What Corps?" Dickey asked.

"Marine Corps," he answered. "Maybe there won't be any more Corps after this."

Dickey had a sudden, chilling thought: Was the United States losing the war?

"I was certain of one conclusion," she wrote: "there was in all the world at this moment only one story: the men fighting and dying on Iwo Jima."

Dickey wanted to get closer to that story. She and the nurses traveled from Hawaii to Guam, where the teletype printer in the correspondent's room was directly linked to a ship just off

Iwo Jima. Dickey watched as one communication clicked in: INCOMPLETE CASUALTY REPORTS INDICATE THAT FOR ONE OUT OF TEN AMERICANS WHO CHARGED ASHORE HERE THERE HAS BEEN NO SUNRISE. THEY DID NOT SURVIVE.

"Poetic, isn't he, this morning?" muttered one correspondent. Those numbers, he said, would certainly be censored; most Americans would never hear about this enormous loss of life.

Another report clicked in: AN UNCONFIRMED RUMOR IS SWEEPING THE SHIP THAT THE FLAG HAS BEEN SIGHTED ON THE TOP OF THE HIGHEST POINT OF THE SAVAGELY CONTESTED SOIL.

A discouraged correspondent in the room said it must be a bad joke.

The teletype machine began again: IT HAS BEEN OFFICIALLY CONFIRMED THAT THE FLAG OF THE UNITED STATES NOW FLIES FROM MOUNT SURIBACHI HIGHEST POINT OF THIS VOLCANIC ISLAND.

The depressed atmosphere in the press room was instantly transformed. The battle was by no means over, but claiming the island's highest point—and a concentrated area of Japanese defenses—was significant, strategically and symbolically; it was the first time during this war that the United States had raised an American flag on Japanese soil. "Now that I was sure it was all right for a correspondent to show emotion," Dickey wrote, "I wiped my eyes with my knuckles."

On the following morning, Dickey was headed for Iwo Jima aboard the USS *Samaritan*, a hospital ship as long as a city block, four decks high, and painted white with red crosses.

Because the purpose of the enormous ship was so clearly identified, Dickey was surprised when they were all drilled for possible enemy attack. Weren't hospital ships off-limits? Dickey was even more surprised when she awoke the next morning to the announcement, "A Japanese bomber type aircraft has just began a run on this ship. . . . We are the target. All hands take cover."

★★★

TWO FLAGS, TWO PHOTOS

The photographers at Iwo Jima had no doubt that a photo of the US flag flying on top of Mount Suribachi had tremendous potential to inspire Americans to stay behind the war effort. But there were actually two US flag-raisings and two major photos. After someone complained that the first flag was too small, it was taken down and immediately replaced with a larger flag. Photographer Joe Rosenthal, who had climbed up the mountain to photograph the first flag, got there just in time to photograph the second flag-raising. The photo was so dramatic—and became so famous, much more so than the first photo—many people mistakenly thought it had been staged for Rosenthal's benefit.

Photo of the first flag-raising on Iwo Jima; US marine Jimmy Michels in the foreground.
Louis R. Lowery, USMC, courtesy of Betty Michels McMahon

★★★

The pilot's first bomb landed too far away. As he came in for a second attempt, an American destroyer shot him down.

After they anchored off Iwo Jima, Dickey watched the "shapeless dirty bloody green bundles"—that is, the wounded—being carried aboard. "Some part of my mind," she wrote, "warned me that if I thought of them as people, just once, I'd be unable to take any more pictures." But she had to take pictures: she was the only photographer on board. If she didn't, "the story of their anguish would never be told since there was no one else here to tell it."

She forced herself toward one of the stretchers. She hadn't yet looked into the face of a wounded man except through a camera lens. She put her camera down and looked straight at this man. Both of his legs were partially destroyed, and covering his mouth was a cardboard tag that read "urgent." Dickey moved it so he could breathe more easily.

He tried to smile his thanks. Dickey asked him how he felt.

"I—feel—lucky."

Dickey asked him why.

"Because—I'm here. Off—the beach," he answered. He told her how the medical corpsmen carried him three miles after he was wounded. "Makes a guy feel lucky."

"After that," Dickey wrote, "I looked squarely at each Marine as I photographed him. As the hours passed, I learned that the one thing almost every man who could talk said was just what Martin had said: I'm lucky. I am alive. I am here."

The USS *Samaritan* held a dangerous secret: severely wounded Japanese prisoners were being taken on board. This was extremely rare: most Japanese military men fought to the death whenever possible, which was why the fighting on Iwo Jima was so fierce and why so many Americans were being killed there. The medics threatened Dickey with jail time if she

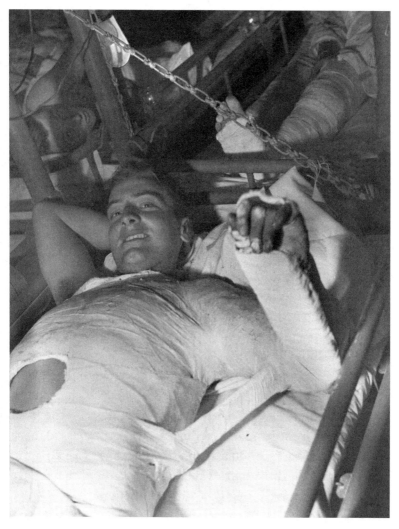

Wounded men aboard the USS *Samaritan. Dickey Chapelle collection, Wisconsin Historical Society, Image #85407*

told anyone about these prisoners. That is, they warned, if she didn't get killed in the riot that would surely occur if the secret got out.

The medics tried to bring the Japanese on board when they would not be seen by any of the wounded Americans, especially those who could walk. But their plans went very wrong. Suddenly 20 wounded American marines were standing on the gangway while behind them on the deck, in plain sight, laid out on stretchers, were several wounded Japanese prisoners.

Dickey watched as a young medic grew pale with fear. "The situation was so unlikely," she wrote, "that at first the Marines did not grasp it." She lifted her camera. "It was suddenly heavier than it had ever been before. A voice hammered inside of me, *Please God . . . no! I don't want to take this picture.*"

A large marine wearing a bloodstained jacket, his left arm in a sling, moved quickly toward the nearest Japanese soldier.

Dickey saw one of the medics move too, a pistol in his hand. But the marine was closer. "His hand," Dickey wrote, "went toward his hip where his trench knife was slung. Then the hand came away from his dungaree pocket. Out of it he took something long and white."

It wasn't a knife. It was a cigarette. "The wounded Marine put the cigarette between the wounded enemy's cracked lips and wordlessly lit it," wrote Dickey. "When he saw the jerky stirrings under the blanket that the man was powerless to move his hands, the Marine squatted on his heels and with an air of boredom removed the butt, waited impassively till the Jap had blown out the smoke, then gave him another drag."

"From the head of the gangway came a rasping voice, 'Okay, okay—*move!*'"

The wounded marine stood up, walked away, and didn't look back.

Dickey then visited a crude tent hospital where doctors struggled to save lives with very little equipment. As she took

★★

THE ENEMY ON IWO

One US marine, Patrick Caruso, said that his opinion of the Japanese changed after fighting them at Iwo Jima. "We had a gross misconception of the enemy before we encountered them," he said. "They were not jokes; they were not inept. We hated them enough to kill them, but we did respect their ability. I often thought that if we had to go to war again, I would want them on our side."

★★

pictures, she noticed one seriously wounded marine watching her. He finally spoke.

"You don't have a gun," he said.

Dickey told him that correspondents didn't carry weapons.

He offered Dickey his trench knife.

"Here, you take it," he said. "Where I'm going I won't need one."

He watched as she fastened the knife's leather sheaf to her own belt. Then he said, "I feel better about you now."

Dickey stumbled out of the tent quickly; she didn't want the marine to see how much his gesture had moved her. Outside she met two officers, a captain and a lieutenant, surprised to see a woman. After explaining who she was, the lieutenant asked her where she wanted to go.

Once again, she replied, "Far forward as you'll let me."

Dickey could barely control her excitement when the lieutenant agreed to take her to "the front." She would soon be taking photos of the most important, most violent battle of the Pacific War.

So she was puzzled when, 40 minutes later, he stopped the truck in a desolate, quiet area of volcanic ash ridges. This was the front? She climbed to the top of the empty ridge, took some photos, and left.

Back on Guam that evening, Dickey discussed her day with Barbara Finch, a more experienced war correspondent. Barbara was surprised the front had been so quiet.

"Tell me every sound you heard," she said.

"A tank fired once," Dickey replied. "A man shouted . . . and there were wasps and I could hear the shutter of my camera click."

"There were what?" Barbara asked.

"Wasps, I guess. Insect noises anyhow."

Marines climbing a ridge on Iwo Jima (photo not taken by Dickey Chapelle). *Attributed to Louis R. Lowery, USMC, courtesy of Betty Michels McMahon*

Barbara smiled. "I don't think we'll file that the entire front was wholly inactive today, after all. And—I guess somebody will have to tell you. There is-no-insect life on Iwo Jima. It's a dead volcano."

"You mean, those weren't—"

"They were not wasps."

Dickey had come under direct Japanese sniper fire.

A few weeks later, on April 1, 1945, Dickey accompanied the large fleet of US ships headed for Okinawa. She was the only nonmedical female in the entire fleet and the only reporter on her hospital ship, the USS *Relief.*

After the men had disembarked, the nurses—and Dickey—waited on the ship for the casualties—who didn't come. After several days, none of the 60,000 Americans—the initial invasion force—had been fired on. What were the Japanese up to?

Dickey wasn't content to find out secondhand. She managed to get verbal permission to go ashore, just for the day. Her stated mission was to photograph blood deliveries and transfusions in order to help Americans back home understand the importance of blood donations. If no blood-related work was occurring on the ship, Dickey would look for it at the nearest field hospital.

When Dickey stepped onto the shore, she realized two things. First, she had again fulfilled her editor's request to be "first someplace": she was now the first woman reporter to set foot on Okinawa during this battle.

Second, she knew she was in trouble. When the driver of the amphibious tractor dropped her off, he told Dickey he would be unable to return for her that evening; the increasingly strong winds were whipping up the surf.

But a few hours later, more than bad weather kept Dickey from obeying orders; the Japanese started to fight. Sniper fire on land and mass kamikaze attacks on the US fleet offshore by waves of Japanese planes made it too dangerous for her to even consider returning to the ship.

When the commanding officers at Okinawa learned there was a female correspondent onshore, they were united in their disapproval; they assumed the marines would needlessly get themselves killed trying to protect her.

But for the moment, they couldn't do anything about it. Dickey was basically left on her own to try to make the most of her situation.

The kamikaze attacks stunned her. "No experience in combat which I have ever known," Dickey wrote later, "is quite like standing before *kamikazes*, feeling the incredible relentless paralysis at the sight of a fellow human being in the dive which must inevitably end in at least his own death."

Dickey also found her way into a crude field hospital, where a man with a serious chest wound waited for an operation. "Anybody would know," she wrote later, "a human being couldn't breathe with such a wound. But the Marine was breathing."

She offered to hold a flashlight during the operation; anything brighter might attract the attention of Japanese snipers. Two hours later, when the operation was finally over, Dickey's arms wouldn't stop shaking. She looked at the wounded marine, now breathing more naturally. "How can he stand it?" she asked aloud to no one in particular.

"Oh," the surgeon replied, as he tossed an empty bottle of blood into the trash, "the limit of human endurance has never been reached."

When it was considered safe enough, Dickey was escorted back to the ship under armed guard. She was stripped of her accreditation. The army put her on a plane for her home in New York City, where her editor wouldn't even publish her photos, claiming that "the wounded looked too—dirty."

Despite all these discouraging events, Dickey was convinced she had become a war correspondent. She was determined to find a way back to "the front," preferably with the US marines.

She was with them when she died.

After spending several decades traveling around the world as a successful photojournalist, Dickey landed in Vietnam to report on the war there. On November 4, 1965, while on a patrol, the marine just ahead of her tripped on a wire attached to a mortar shell and a hand grenade. A piece of shrapnel from the explosion hit Dickey in the neck and severed her carotid artery. She died

★★

KAMIKAZES

The Japanese used kamikaze ("divine wind") suicide attacks—small planes carrying explosives flown directly into an enemy target—increasingly toward the end of the war, but in the greatest numbers and with the most effect at Okinawa, where they sank 30 ships and damaged many more. Most of the kamikaze pilots feared their impending suicide flights less than the ostracism and family shame they would receive if they didn't accept their mission. And all were promised that their souls would enjoy eternal honor at the Yasukuni shrine in Tokyo. While their example was used to inspire Japanese civilians for the impending ground invasion, kamikazes had a damaging psychological effect on the Allies, who viewed these attacks as chillingly personal.

★★

within minutes, becoming the first female American correspondent to be killed in action.

The news of her death "passed like wildfire" through the entire marine company. A group of marines personally escorted her remains back to the United States. In the year after Dickey's death, marines built a dispensary in South Vietnam and dedicated it to her. A marble plaque outside read, "To the memory of Dickey Chapelle, war correspondent, killed in action near here on 4 November 1965. She was one of us and we will miss her."

While conducting the dedication ceremony, marine corps general Lewis Walt recalled a conversation he had with Dickey shortly before her death. When she told him she was going on patrol the following day, he warned her to "be careful and to keep her head down."

She replied, "When my time comes, I want it to be on a patrol with the marines."

LEARN MORE

Dickey Chapelle Under Fire: Photographs by the First American Female War Correspondent Killed in Action by John Garofolo (Wisconsin Historical Society Press, 2015).

"Legendary War Photographer Dickey Chapelle Back in Focus" by Meg Jones, *Milwaukee Journal Sentinel*, October 17, 2014, www.jsonline.com/news/milwaukee/legendary-war-photographer-dickey-chapelle-back-in-focus-b99371912z1-279644882.html.

War, Women, and the News: How Female Journalists Won the Battle to Cover World War II by Catherine Gourley (Atheneum Books for Young Readers, 2007).

What's a Woman Doing Here? A Reporter's Report on Herself by Dickey Chapelle (William Morrow, 1962).

Where the Action Was: Women War Correspondents in World War II by Penny Colman (Random House, 2002).

EPILOGUE

ON JUNE 22, 1945, the United States claimed victory on Okinawa, the latest in a series of US victories over Japanese-controlled islands in the South Pacific. Approximately 70,000 Okinawan civilians lost their lives during this battle, many of them in mass suicides: the Japanese military had convinced them that taking their own lives was preferable to the horrors awaiting them at the hands of the victorious Americans.

At this point, over 300,000 Japanese civilians living in 66 Japanese cities had also been killed in Allied bombing raids. These attacks were designed to accomplish Japan's surrender, an unconditional surrender in which the defeated nation could have no say in the terms.

The leaders of Japan—a group of military officers and politicians together referred to as the Big Six—had no intention of surrendering unconditionally, no matter how many of their citizens were killed; it would be an unbearable loss of honor. So while Japanese civilians continued to die by the thousands, the nation geared up for the inevitable land invasion by the Americans. With the United States in control of Okinawa, only 400 miles south of the Japanese home, it would not be long.

"One Hundred Million Die Together"

American code breakers intercepted multiple messages proving Japanese leaders were preparing their nation to fight to the death: Japan's national slogan at this point was "One Hundred Million Die Together." They prepared thousands of vessels—both airplanes and submarines—for suicide missions against the impending US invasion fleet of ships. The Americans who weren't blown up before landing onshore would face armed

Japanese students receiving weapons training, 1945. *Wikimedia Commons*

forces that now included teenagers and old men, along with female civilians, some of whom were being trained with real weapons, others with crude spears.

Survivors of the fierce fighting on Iwo Jima and Okinawa knew that the number of American servicemen killed during a ground invasion of the Japanese home islands would be staggering. The US government scrambled to manufacture thousands of additional Purple Heart medals—the award for being wounded or killed during combat; Military strategists estimated American deaths and wounded during the invasion would total at least 250,000 each.

Japanese military leaders, long aware they couldn't defeat the United States in direct battle, hoped these invasion casualties would make Americans tire of the war quickly. This was their only hope: perhaps then they would receive terms of surrender they considered acceptable.

Japan knew its enemy well. The United States was already war-weary. It had recently helped defeat Germany and was now chasing down Nazi war criminals. It was assisting the flood of European refugees uprooted by the war. And one of its war allies was a ruthless tyrant.

Josef Stalin and the Iron Curtain

Allied leaders suspected that Josef Stalin, head of the Communist Soviet Union, had murdered millions of his own people before the war. But without his army battling the Germans on the Eastern Front, the Allies would never have defeated Adolf Hitler. And while Stalin clearly didn't care about the lives of his people, he was very concerned about gaining more territory. So as his reward for the heavy Soviet losses on Germany's Eastern Front—approximately 7 million soldiers and 13 million civilians—he demanded control of nations in Eastern Europe from his allies, promising democratic elections in each nation, elections that never took place. After the war, in 1946, Winston Churchill would use the term "iron curtain" to describe what Stalin had done in Eastern Europe, saying that "an Iron Curtain has descended across the Continent."

Would an "iron curtain" also descend across the Far East? Stalin's allies had earlier asked him to pledge his support in a war against Japan within three months of Germany's defeat. In the spring of 1945, when it became clear the war with Germany was nearly won, the Soviets suddenly declared, one year early, that their five-year nonaggression pact with Japan was over. For months, 1,600,000 Soviet troops had been massing on the border between the Soviet Union and Japanese-controlled Manchuria. Was Stalin preparing to help his allies defeat Japan? Was he simply planning to seize Japanese territory for himself before that defeat? Or both?

In the midst of this turmoil and uncertainty, on July 26, 1945, US president Harry Truman issued a proposal, signed by Winston Churchill of Britain and Chiang Kai-shek of China, that made plain the terms for a Japanese surrender.

The Potsdam Declaration

The proposal, called the Potsdam Declaration, promised that if Japan would surrender unconditionally, the victors would immediately restore ordinary Japanese soldiers and sailors to civilian life unharmed, bring war criminals to trial, destroy Japan's ability to make war, strengthen the Japanese economy, and overturn the current government and replace it with one chosen by the Japanese people. The Allies would occupy Japan only until these changes were made. If Japan refused, the alternative would be "prompt and utter destruction."

Although there were three signatures on the declaration, the Big Six knew the United States was basically spearheading this invasion alone. While the British and the French were also in the Far East, supporting the United States effort in a limited way, they were more involved with attempts to reclaim their colonial possessions.

Furthermore, Churchill was defeated in a national election on the same day of the Potsdam Declaration. And Chiang Kai-shek's Nationalist government was weary and corrupt, its large armies disorganized and ill-equipped. Because Chiang had refused to surrender to Japan against impossible odds, he had kept Japanese troops mired in China since 1937. This is largely why his allies considered him China's leader. But was he really? Individual warlords, answering to no one, remained in control of certain areas as they had throughout the war. Three puppet regimes, set up by the Japanese, contained a total of 1.5 million Chinese military men. And the influence of Mao Zedong's Communist forces was growing as they watched and waited for their opportunity to seize all of China.

Josef Stalin had not even been asked to sign the declaration; the Soviet Union was not at war with Japan. Japanese officials clung to the feeble hope that the Soviets might help them obtain better terms of surrender from the Allies; they worked feverishly to make this happen. The Soviet responses were always vague enough to offer them a tiny ray of hope.

The Big Six decided to ignore the Potsdam Declaration. The Japanese prime minister, knowing that US planes had deluged Japanese cities with copies of the declaration, published Japan's official response in the newspapers: Japan would fight the Declaration by *mokusatsu*, a term that meant "killing with silence." Japan would continue the battle.

So would the United States. With a new, deadly weapon.

The Atomic Bomb

Since 1939, an international team of physicists had been working in the United States on a top secret mission that by 1941 they referred to as the Manhattan Project. They were trying to create a new type of bomb with a powerful explosion caused by the fission, or splitting, of a uranium atom. Their urgent motive was to beat physicists working on the same project in Nazi Germany; German physicists had first discovered the idea in late 1938. The news soon spread throughout the international scientific community, including to refugees from Europe living in the United States. The most famous of those refugees—Albert Einstein—personally informed President Franklin Roosevelt about the threat of a Nazi atomic bomb. What Hitler could do with such a weapon was unthinkable.

But he never got a chance to use it; Nazi Germany was defeated before its scientists developed the bomb. The Manhattan Project physicists wondered if they should continue their work. Most definitely, said President Truman; the war with Japan was still on. On July 16, 1945, the physicists set off the first successful atomic explosion device in the deserts of New Mexico.

A few days before the release of the Potsdam Declaration, plans were made—in case Japan refused the terms—to drop an atomic bomb on a Japanese city. Hiroshima was chosen as the first target. It was one of the largest Japanese cities not yet affected by the firebombing campaigns. It was also a military headquarters; dropping the bomb there had the potential to hinder the Japanese war effort.

US leaders realized that in addition to killing or wounding about 43,000 Japanese soldiers housed at Hiroshima, the bomb would also kill civilians—thousands of them.

By the end of the war, the Allies considered enemy casualties an unfortunate necessity of battle. Before Nazi Germany surrendered, the United States and Great Britain had bombed many heavily populated German cities, killing approximately 300,000 civilians. During the Allied firebombings in Dresden alone, 21,000 to 40,000 German civilians lost their lives.

Now the United States prepared to unleash a weapon—a bomb the physicists named Little Boy—that would kill everything and everyone in its path within 1,000 yards.

On the morning of August 6, 15-year-old Hiroshima resident Yamaoka Michiko was walking to her job as a telephone operator for the military. The desperate, determined Japanese government had ordered teenagers out of school and into the war effort. Michiko's mother warned her that an American B-29— the type of plane always involved with firebombings (referred to by the Japanese as *B-san* or Mr. B)—had been spotted. Michiko wasn't worried. She had been told Japan was winning the war; the Japanese people "only had to endure" until their inevitable victory was achieved.

Suddenly, there was a powerful silence. Michiko sensed "something strong," something "terribly intense." She felt as if she were floating. She thought she was going to die. She whispered good-bye to her mother. Then she fell unconscious.

Michiko woke under a pile of rubble. She couldn't move. Her mother, familiar with her route to work, was calling out for her. When Michiko called back, her mother convinced some soldiers to dig her out.

When she was free of the rubble, Michiko saw that her clothes and skin were burned. She looked at the scene around her, later describing it as "a living hell." There were dead bodies, people with missing limbs, people with burned, swollen faces, others trying to keep their internal organs from falling out. None of them, she said later, "looked like human beings."

Her mother told her to run away; she was going to stay and rescue another relative. On her way, Michiko saw one of her coworkers. She called her name. The young woman didn't respond. When she finally recognized Michiko's voice, the coworker said, "Miss Yamaoka, you look like a monster!" Michiko's face had temporarily swollen beyond recognition.

Because Michiko was some distance away from the center of the destruction, she survived her injuries (although she would suffer from the bomb's effects for the rest of her life). Of the approximately 70,000 people immediately killed by Little Boy, those at the center of the impact were simply vaporized by the bomb's 5,000-degree heat, some leaving only shadows of their bodies etched in the concrete sidewalks. Thousands who survived the initial blast would die by the end of the year from radiation poisoning.

Hours after the bomb fell, President Truman issued a formal statement to the Japanese government, which included the following:

It was to spare the Japanese people from utter destruction that the ultimatum of July 26 was issued at Potsdam. Their leaders promptly rejected that ultimatum. If they do not now accept our terms they may expect a rain of ruin from the air, the like of which has never been seen on this earth.

Japan's Big Six took stock of Hiroshima's damage. Although the center of Hiroshima was completely flattened, not all of them were convinced it was the result of a single bomb. Others didn't believe the United States possessed the number of atomic bombs implied in Truman's phrase, "ruin from the air." If it did, world opinion would certainly prevent the United States from dropping more. While the political leaders urged surrender, the generals refused.

They issued no formal response to the new warning.

Meanwhile, they waited hopefully for a clear communication from the Soviet Union.

In the early hours of August 9, they received one. The Soviet army launched an attack on Manchuria. Stalin, who had received information about the Manhattan Project from physicists on the team, was secretly furious the United States had beaten the Soviet Union in obtaining a functional atomic bomb. He was determined to gain as much Japanese-controlled territory as possible before the war ended.

A few hours later, the United States dropped a second atomic bomb, which they called Fat Man, on Nagasaki, a populous city heavily involved in war production. The bomb immediately killed 40,000 people. Again, thousands more wounded would die by the end of the year.

The Big Six held multiple urgent meetings to debate Japan's next move. The politicians urged surrender, while most of the generals were still determined to fight, one of them saying, "There is really no alternative for us but to continue the war. . . . We must fight to the end no matter how great the odds against us!"

Emperor Hirohito

Shortly before midnight, the last of these meetings included Emperor Michinomiya Hirohito. He stood up and gave a short speech that read in part, "I cannot bear to see my innocent people suffer any longer. Ending the war is the only way to restore world peace and to relieve the nation from the terrible distress with which it is burdened . . . the time has come when we must bear the unbearable."

Then he walked out. While his words caused a shock to many in the room, they did not spur immediate plans for surrender. The battle between Soviet and Japanese forces raged in Manchuria. The United States resumed the firebombing of Japanese cities as the Big Six debated Japan's destiny far into the night.

When they finally agreed to honor the wishes of their divine emperor, Hirohito decided to take another step toward peace: he recorded a speech in the imperial palace that he wanted broadcast to the Japanese people. In it, he urged surrender, explaining that Japan had begun the war with the United States and Britain "out of Our sincere desire to assure Japan's self-preservation and the stabilization of East Asia."

He praised the efforts of his military and civilians but said that after four long years, "the war situation has developed not necessarily to Japan's advantage." The rest of the world had turned against them. And "the enemy" was now using "a new and most cruel bomb"; to continue the war would not only cause the destruction of Japan but would "lead to the total extinction of human civilization."

A group of Japanese army officers were determined that this message would never be broadcast. On the evening of August 14, in what would be called the Kyūjō Incident, they killed the commander of the palace guards and seized control of the imperial palace for several hours in order to locate and destroy the recording so the war would continue.

They failed to find it. And on the following day, the Japanese people heard the voice of their emperor for the first time. His speech was called *"Gyokuon-hōsō"* or the "Jewel Voice Broadcast." Although the speech was difficult to understand, its intention was clear. Hirohito's message was greeted with shock, dismay, and many suicides. But it brought about Japan's official surrender.

Defeat and Occupation

August 15, 1945, was declared V-J, or Victory over Japan, Day. And on September 2, 1945, with US general Douglas MacArthur presiding and representatives from many Allied nations in attendance, Japanese officials came aboard the USS *Missouri*, anchored in Tokyo Bay, and signed the terms for Japan's unconditional surrender.

The Japanese people, shocked at their defeat, occupied by American forces, and attempting to rebuild their lives in the midst of a devastated economy, did not connect their suffering to the actions of their wartime leaders. There was little national discussion on why Japan initiated the war and why it was ultimately defeated. It was as if the war had simply happened to them, like some sort of natural disaster.

The war crimes trials did little to help Japanese civilians accept the reality of what their military had done, perhaps because many of the trials were held not in Japan but in the countries where Japanese soldiers had abused and killed their populations. The trial held in Tokyo lasted so long—almost two and a half years—that many Japanese civilians lost interest in its proceedings.

Approximately 1,000 war criminals were executed or died in prison. The names of all these men were eventually included at the Yasukuni shrine, which, it is believed, enshrines the souls of Japanese military men who died in the service of their country. Although Emperor Hirohito refused to visit the shrine after these names were added, the Yasukuni shrine is regularly and publicly visited by many prominent Japanese officials to this day.

While neo-Nazis have always openly admired Nazi war criminals, it's difficult to imagine modern Germany's politicians honoring the memory of these men in any way. Why the difference? Some of it has to do with how Japan and Germany were treated by the United States after the war.

When Japanese officials were signing the surrender aboard the USS *Missouri*, the occupying Allies were running a denazification program in Germany. Months earlier, when the Allies began liberating the concentration camps, American generals

★★

THE EMPEROR AND THE WAR

While Hitler gave direct orders to German military leaders during World War II, this doesn't seem to have been true of Emperor Hirohito and the Japanese military. He was considered an actual deity by his people. Although he was kept informed of the wartime activities of his military-run government, even its atrocities, many historians believe he was more of a national symbol who rubber stamped or ratified his military's prior decisions, instead of actually initiating them himself. However, because his actions eventually brought about Japan's surrender, some argue that if he had spoken up earlier, he might have prevented the atrocities or even the war itself. One reason, perhaps, that his role has remained murky is that during the time between the surrender and the US occupation, thousands of government documents—some of them, perhaps linking Hirohito to criminal responsibility—were deliberately destroyed by Japanese officials. Others remain sealed to this day.

★★

forced German civilians who lived near the camps to view the piles of starved corpses, before burying them. The international presses were invited to photograph and film these horrific findings. As a result of these and similar efforts, there were few postwar Germans who could deny the Holocaust.

The Allies offered no such deprogramming assistance to the Japanese people. Many lower-level convicted war criminals eventually had their sentences shortened. Emperor Hirohito, who many Americans considered a war criminal, was never brought to trial and was also allowed to retain his throne. While this brought a welcome sense of stability to the Japanese people—which is why MacArthur refused to try him even when Hirohito offered to take the stand—it also helped prevent them from coming to terms with their national guilt.

Why did the United States treat the Japanese in a gentler manner than it did the Germans? They realized their old enemy could be a new ally in a new war.

The Cold War

Stalin was furious that the United States made peace with Japan without including him—he was hoping to bring down his Communist iron curtain on part of the defeated nation. He had already seized North Korea and other Asian territories Russia had owned during the 19th century. But it wasn't enough.

His alliance with America and Britain was over. The Cold War—in which the United States and the Soviet Union sought to limit the global influence of the other from behind a growing stockpile of nuclear weapons—would soon begin.

And the Soviet Union was not the only powerful Communist nation in the east. On October 1, 1949, Chiang Kai-shek's Nationalist forces were officially defeated by the Communist forces of Mao Zedong. China—or the People's Republic of China, as it was now called—was officially Communist.

Western nations saw Communism as a threat that loomed in other areas of the Far East as well, prompting US president Dwight Eisenhower in 1954 to refer to those nations as a series of dominoes in danger of falling to Communism. Helping Japan become a bulwark against the spread of Communism in the Far East was now considered so urgent by the US government that if some concessions regarding its past had to be made, so be it.

Recovery, Denial, and Remembrance

Japan's rapid economic recovery—with generous American assistance—eventually transformed it into the most prosperous nation in the Far East. But as the years passed, Japan's neighbors became increasingly dismayed by what they considered halfhearted apologies and an unwillingness to pay significant war reparations to help rebuild economies the now prosperous nation had once shattered.

Despite the efforts of many contemporary Japanese individuals calling for a full exploration of their nation's wartime actions, a surprising number of their fellow citizens energetically deny this part of their history or resent all mention of the topic. Japanese students are taught that the Allied oil embargoes gave Japan no choice but to go to war in 1941, yet they learn next to nothing about the aggression and atrocities their military committed in China that brought on that embargo.

Even throughout Western nations, very little is understood about the approximately six million unarmed victims—civilians and prisoners of war—deliberately killed by Imperial Japan's military during World War II. These victims, like those of the Nazi Holocaust, should never be forgotten. Neither should those who tried to do something to help: people whose choices transformed them from victim to hero and whose stories of courage in the midst of extreme misery will long have the power to inspire.

ACKNOWLEDGMENTS

WHEN I WAS FIRST contacted by *America: Fact vs. Fiction* for an interview regarding American women's contributions to World War II, the questions they sent made me wonder if there might be enough documentation on heroic women of the Pacific War to fill a young adult collective biography. It turns out there was, so I'm indebted to them and also to Chicago Review Press for green-lighting this project.

I'd like to thank the following specialists for their invaluable input: Mary Cronk Farrell, expert on the American Bataan/Corregidor nurses and author of *Pure Grit*; Dr. Theresa Kaminski, historian and author of *Angels of the Underground*; the late Betty McIntosh, journalist and OSS agent; Andre B. Sobocinski, historian at the US Navy Bureau of Medicine; John Tewell, expert on World War II history in the Philippines; Sig Unander, Claire Phillips expert; and Dr. Meredith Veldman, historian at Louisiana State University.

Every history author should have a few brilliant, well-read, historically inclined friends. Mine are Bob Blomquist and Ed Sketch. I'm honored by their friendship and grateful for their willingness to review and comment on the nonnarrative portions of the book.

A new friend, Dr. Robert Messer, associate professor emeritus of 20th-century US history at the University of Illinois at Chicago, put his heart and soul into providing me with valuable food for thought regarding the war's beginning and end, then agreed to review the entire manuscript while thoroughly answering many questions along the way. Our communications made me sorry I missed the opportunity to hear his lectures, as they must have been quite fascinating.

I'm grateful to the following people who agreed to review the most potentially disturbing material and who provided me with many valuable insights: Dr. Alex Baugh, teacher and author of *The Children's War Blog*; Katie King, teen bibliophile extraordinaire; Pat Miller Mathews, MLS, former book reviewer for *The Bulletin of the Center for Children's Books*; Lesley Munro, MAEd, head of history at Homewood School in Kent, England; Ana Peso, MS, library and information science, and MEd, librarian at Glenbrook High School in Northbrook, Illinois; and Samantha Shank, teen history buff and blogger at *Le Chaim on the Right*.

My brilliant husband, John, got off easy this time around: he had no French-to-English translation work as he did with all my previous books. But I'd like to thank him for being an invaluable sounding board and for reading through the finished manuscript before it went off to the publisher. I can't imagine doing otherwise.

DISCUSSION QUESTIONS AND SUGGESTIONS FOR FURTHER STUDY

What caused Peggy Hull (chapter 1) to change her opinion about war correspondence?

What was one particular reason Peggy Hull (chapter 1) was hoping to travel with the planned ground invasion of the Japanese home islands?

Why wasn't Elizabeth MacDonald's Pearl Harbor report (chapter 4) published at the time she wrote it?

Explain how the "black propaganda" Elizabeth MacDonald created (chapter 4) may have affected the outcome of the fighting in the Burma campaign.

How did Claire Phillips (chapter 8) improve the relief work Margaret Utinsky had started (chapter 6)? Why did both of these women take on false identities?

Why was Sybil Kathigasu's husband (chapter 10) initially reluctant to operate on a wounded guerrilla?

Why didn't Sybil Kathigasu (chapter 10) take the guerrilla's offer to escape certain arrest?

Why were there so many Chinese guerrillas in Malaya (chapter 10)?

Why didn't Elizabeth Choy (chapter 11) recommend any Kempeitai officers for the death penalty?

Why did Vivian Bullwinkel's fellow nurses (chapter 12) in the internment camp keep her survival story a secret?

Why was the vocal orchestra in chapter 13 not simply called a choir?

What was the Japanese reaction to the vocal orchestra?

Explain how the Bataan Death March initiated and energized the Filipino resistance.

What major decision was made at the Arcadia Conference (chapter 5), and why were the Bataan defenders not told about it?

Explain how the Rescission Act (chapter 7) motivated Yay Panlilio to gear her memoir toward American readers.

Why do you think Filipino guerrilla leader Marking (chapter 7) was initially hostile to the idea of working with the Americans?

In chapter 5, why were the Japanese surprised to encounter American nurses at Corregidor?

Why is it remarkable that the nurses at Bataan and Corregidor (chapter 5) performed so well under fire?

Why do you think the Japanese singled out Chinese civilians living in such places as Malaya (chapter 10) and Singapore (chapter 11) for particularly cruel treatment?

Why was Jane Kendeigh (chapter 14) photographed so much during the war? How did she react to her sudden fame?

Discuss why Jane Kendeigh's landing on a battlefield (chapter 14) was celebrated but Dickey Chapelle's (chapter 15) was not.

Explain how the Pearl Harbor attack led to Executive Order #9066, imprisoning all West Coast Japanese Americans.

Explain precisely how Executive Order #9066 denied West Coast Japanese Americans their constitutional rights.

How did the fighting on Iwo Jima and Okinawa directly affect the way in which the war ended?

Read *The Flamboya Tree: A Family's War-Time Courage* by Clara Olink Kelly and *I Have Lived a Thousand Years: Growing Up in the Holocaust* by Livia Bitton-Jackson. How were the camps for women run by the German SS different from those run by the Japanese military ? How were they the same?

Read *Looking Like the Enemy: My Story of Imprisonment in Japanese-American Prison Camps* by Mary Matsuda Gruenewald and *The Flamboya Tree: A Family's War-Time Courage* by Clara Olink Kelly. Compare and contrast the experiences of Mary and Clara and explain how their mothers helped them cope.

Compare the memoirs of the following Japanese Americans: Mary Matsuda Gruenewald in *Looking Like the Enemy: My Story of Imprisonment in Japanese-American Prison Camps* and Jeanne Wakatsuki Houston in *Farewell to Manzanar*. How did their fathers make a difference, for good or bad, in their experiences?

Compare and contrast the experiences and reportage of World War II correspondents Dickey Chapelle (chapter 15); Margaret Bourke-White (*Reporting Under Fire: 16 Daring Women War Correspondents and Photojournalists*); and Martha Gellhorn (*Reporting Under Fire* and *Women Heroes of World War II: 26 Stories of Espionage, Sabotage, Resistance, and Rescue*). How did these correspondents overcome the gender-based hurdles placed in their way?

Explain specifically how being an entertainer facilitated the work of the following wartime spies: Claire Phillips (chapter 8) and Josephine Baker (*The Many Faces of Josephine Baker: Dancer, Singer, Activist, Spy*).

Compare and contrast the experiences of the following US military nurses: Jane Kendeigh (chapter 14) and Muriel Engelman (*Women Heroes of World War II: 26 Stories of Espionage, Sabotage, Resistance, and Rescue*).

Virginia Hall and Marlene Dietrich (*Women Heroes of World War II: 26 Stories of Sabotage, Espionage, Resistance, and Rescue*) and Elizabeth MacDonald McIntosh (chapter 4), all worked for the OSS during World War II. Compare and contrast their specific work.

Read the imprisonment portion of *Unbroken (The Young Adult Adaptation): An Olympian's Journey from Airman to Castaway to Captive* by Laura Hillenbrand, especially pages 171–224. Compare and contrast the experiences of Louis Zamperini with that of the imprisoned women in this book, especially Sybil Kathigasu (chapter 10).

How did Fascism—a single-party political system intolerant of dissention—differ in Japan and Germany during World War II? Discuss the causes of its growth in each nation, how it was implemented, and how/why Fascism propelled both nations to initiate war.

How did Germany's invasion of Western Europe in the spring of 1940 affect the Japanese government?

Explain how the Tripartite Pact was a direct warning to the United States to remain neutral in the war.

Compare and contrast the Japanese Kempeitai with the German Gestapo.

Every German student must learn about Hitler and Nazism while Japanese students learn very little about their nation's role in the war. Why?

Why did the Japanese military not adhere to the Geneva Convention as regards treatment of POWs?

Explain how racism was the foundation for how Japanese soldiers treated their fellow Asians.

What major issue caused offense to the Japanese delegates during the Paris Peace Conference in 1919?

Why did Japan's Co-Prosperity Sphere at first sound like a good idea to Asians in the Far East? Was it a lie, or do you think the Japanese truly believed their Asian neighbors would be better off under their domination?

Why do you think students outside of Asia learn more about the Nazi Holocaust than they do about Pacific War events such as the Nanking Massacre?

Why do you think the atomic bomb attacks on Hiroshima and Nagasaki (which killed approximately 200,000 people, both civilians and military personnel) are more well known than the US firebombing raids on Japan (which killed approximately 300,000 civilians), or the US and British attacks on Germany (which killed approximately 300,000 civilians)?

Watch the following films: *The Great Escape* (NR) and *Unbroken* (PG-13). How were the experiences of Allied POWs, as presented in these films, different in the Pacific War from in the war in Europe? How were they similar?

Suggested Reading on the Topic of Japanese Resistance to Fascism

Because there is no Japanese resister section in this book, you might wonder if there were any Japanese people who tried to work against their wartime government as some Germans did during the Nazi regime. There were some anti-Fascist Japanese, but they were relatively few in number and their memoirs and biographies are even fewer, for reasons I mention in the epilogue.

If you are curious about this topic, however, I found a few English-language books that might be of interest. *Japan at War: An Oral History* describes multiple instances of Japanese people whose thought patterns—and sometimes even their actions— were out of step with the rest of Japanese wartime society.

Restless Wave: My Life in Two Worlds is the fictionalized memoir of Ayako Ishigaki, a young woman who eventually moved to the United States in order to work against the Japanese military regime. Her memoir doesn't cover this period in her life—it ends before Japan's full military involvement in the Far East— but it is still a fascinating glimpse of Japanese culture from the viewpoint of an independently thinking young woman.

The New Sun and *Horizon Is Calling* are two autobiographical picture books—a few words and a line drawing on each page—geared for teens and written by Atsushi Iwamatsu (pen name Taro Yashima). They relate the story of Atsushi and his wife, Tomoe Sasako. This couple protested the Fascist Japanese government during the 1930s, were mistreated and imprisoned by the Kempeitai, and fled together to the United States in 1939. These two books can be difficult to find but are well worth the effort if you can get help from your librarian.

One last book I found on this topic is *Target Tokyo: The Story of the Sorge Spy Ring*. It details the inner workings of a Soviet espionage network in Japan that involved a number of Japanese Communists, a few of them women.

NOTES

Introduction

approximately 300,000 Japanese: Cook, *Japan at War: An Oral History*, 23.

Peggy Hull

"The hapless civilian . . . fate of a soldier": Benjamin, *Eye Witness by Members of the Overseas Press Club of America*, 7.

January, 28, 1932: Mitter, *Forgotten Ally: China's World War II: 1937–1945*, 63–64; Rees, *Horror in the East*, 23–23.

"Go to work": Smith and Bogart, *The Wars of Peggy Hull: The Life and Times of a War Correspondent*, 189.

"In company with other Americans": Chicago *Tribune*, January 29, 1932, quoted on page 190 of *Wars of Peggy Hull* and 151 of Colman, *Adventurous Women: Eight True Stories About Women Who Made a Difference*.

"If you are ever": Smith and Bogart, *Wars of Peggy Hull*, 191.

"His body shook": Benjamin, *Eye Witness*, 4.

"Increasing, deadly resolve": Benjamin, *Eye Witness*, 5.

"Hands began to twist": Benjamin, *Eye Witness*, 6.

"*Like Sasha*": Benjamin, *Eye Witness*, 6–7.

"*In the briefest*": Benjamin, *Eye Witness*, 11.

"*You are lost?*": Benjamin, *Eye Witness*, 12.

"*You know*": Benjamin, *Eye Witness*, 13.

14,000 Chinese: Mitter, *Forgotten Ally*, 64.

"*The mangled bodies of boys*": Smith and Bogart, *Wars of Peggy Hull*, 241.

"*We are not fighting*": *Cleveland Plain Dealer*, May 9, 1944, quoted in Smith and Bogart, *Wars of Peggy Hull*, 248.

"*They were sent*": *Cleveland Plain Dealer*, March 14, 1945, quoted in Smith and Bogart, *Wars of Peggy Hull*, 250.

Minnie Vautrin

"*Are we to*": Diary entry, August 14, 1937.

"*If Japan only*": Diary entry, September 26, 1937.

"*Our fate at*": Diary entry, December 13, 1937.

"*They wanted every*": Diary entry, December 16, 1937.

"*Trust Our Japanese Army*": Chang, *The Rape of Nanking: The Forgotten Holocaust of World War II*, 120.

"*Our officers told us . . . many Chinese*": Ken Wright, *Island of Death*, Military History Online, www.militaryhistoryonline.com/wwii /articles/islandofdeath.aspx.

"*A stream of weary*": Diary entry, December 17, 1937.

"*with a dagger*": Diary entry, December 18, 1937.

"*with horror written*": Diary entry, December 18, 1937.

"*the only thing*": Diary entry, December 18, 1937.

"*In my wrath*": Diary entry, December 19, 1937.

"*There is no need . . . at the end*": Hu, *American Goddess at the Rape of Nanking: The Courage of Minnie Vautrin*, 100.

"*Women do not*": Diary entry, February 1, 1938.

"*Living Goddess*": Hu, *American Goddess*, 106.

"*When they played*": Diary entry, February 8, 1938.

"*At a time when*": Hu, *American Goddess*, 138.

All Minnie Vautrin diary quotes are reprinted by permission of Special Collections, Yale Divinity School Library, Minnie Vautrin papers, film Ms62, Diary of Wilhelmina Vautrin, 1937–1940.

Gladys Aylward

"if you can": Aylward, *The Little Woman*, 82.

"Whether you leave . . . price on your head": Burgess, *The Small Woman: The Heroic Story of Gladys Aylward*, 199.

"You are just saying": Aylward, *Little Woman*, 84.

"Any person giving": Aylward, *Little Woman*, 84.

"After being stopped": Aylward, *Little Woman*, 28.

"The Inn of the Eight Happinesses": Burgess, *Small Woman*, 56.

"Well, if she": Aylward, *Little Woman*, 50.

they'd never seen: Burgess, *Small Woman*, 125.

"Will you help . . . conscience will allow": Burgess, *Small Woman*, 166.

"sometimes leading Nationalist": Burgess, *Small Woman*, 186.

"had despoiled our": Aylward, *Little Woman*, 69.

"Flee ye": Aylward, *Little Woman*, 85.

"No mule will": Aylward, *Little Woman*, 85.

"I would not": Aylward, *Little Woman*, 92.

"Then why does not . . . will be answered": Burgess, *Small Woman*, 224.

"Ai-weh-deh, here's a . . . is a battlefield": Burgess, *Small Woman*, 226.

"Madam . . . across those mountains": Aylward, *Little Woman*, 95.

"For days": Aylward, *Little Woman*, 98.

beheading of 200: Aylward, *Little Woman*, 131–134.

Elizabeth MacDonald

"The islands are under attack . . . real McCoy": Bob Bergen, *OSS Undercover Girl: Elizabeth P. McIntosh, an Interview* (Banana Tree, 2012), Kindle edition, chapter 2.

"a formation . . . rooftop fly into the air": McIntosh, "Honolulu After Pearl Harbor: A Report Published for the First Time, 71 Years Later," *Washington Post*, December 6, 2014, www.washingtonpost .com/opinions/honolulu-after-pearl-harbor-a-report-published -for-the-first-time-71-years-later/2012/12/06/e9029986-3d69-11e2 -bca3-aadc9b7e29c5_story.html.

"that numb terror": McIntosh, "Honolulu."

"The peace of . . . in peril": Hotta, *Japan 1941: Countdown to Infamy*, 10.

"Bombs were still dropping . . . charred bodies of children": McIntosh, "Honolulu."

"The blood-soaked drivers": McIntosh, "Honolulu."
"laid on slabs": McIntosh, "Honolulu."
"blood and the fear": McIntosh, "Honolulu."
"The all-night horror . . . wrapped in fear": McIntosh, "Honolulu."
"In the nightmare of . . . Poison in your food!": McIntosh, "Honolulu."
"Definitely not": MacDonald, *Undercover Girl*, 4.
"Fill them out": MacDonald, *Undercover Girl*, 4.
"the art of influencing": MacDonald, *Undercover Girl*, 2.
"Even the best": MacDonald, *Undercover Girl*, 3.
"Out of twenty": MacDonald, *Undercover Girl*, 8.
"rare, strange personalities": MacDonald, *Undercover Girl*, 9.
"Why can't they be mailed": MacDonald, *Undercover Girl*, 80.
"It's so sad . . . for a lost cause": MacDonald, *Undercover Girl*, 81.
"As the Burma campaign": MacDonald, *Undercover Girl*, 97.
Quotations from *Honolulu: A Report* and *Undercover Girl* published by permission of Elizabeth P. McIntosh.

Denny Williams

420 operations: Williams, *To the Angels*, 57.
while Denny was bathing: Williams, *To the Angels*, 51.
"You are well aware . . . advised to surrender": Williams, *To the Angels*, 54.
"until the bayonet": Williams, *To the Angels*, 54.
"Help is on the way . . . will be destroyed": Norman, *We Band of Angels: The Untold Story of American Nurses Trapped on Bataan by the Japanese*, 36–37.
"There are times": Lukacs, *Escape From Davao: The Forgotten Story of the Most Daring Prison Break of the Pacific War*, 33.
"We're the battling": Michael Norman and Elizabeth M. Norman. *Tears in the Darkness: The Story of the Bataan Death March and its Aftermath* (New York: Farrar, Straus & Giroux, 2009), 128.
While listening to: Lukacs, *Escape from Davao*, 32.
"We were expendable": Williams, *To the Angels*, 66.
"I came through and I shall return": "MacArthur's Speeches: 'I Shall Return,'" American Experience, http://www.pbs.org/wgbh/amex/macarthur/filmmore/reference/primary/macspeech02.html.
"We have the honor . . . any action whatsoever": Norman, *We Band of Angels*, 75.

"Most of us": Williams, *To the Angels*, 71.
"The battle was now": Williams, *To the Angels*, 71–72.
"We're leaving . . . it's inevitable": Williams, *To the Angels*, 76–77.
"by blocking out": Williams, *To the Angels*, 88.
"no nurse voiced": Williams, *To the Angels*, 95.
"Compared to Bataan": Williams, *To the Angels*, 97.
"the Japanese were": Williams, *To the Angels*, 114.
"Denny, Denny are you . . . cut off": Williams, *To the Angels*, 117–118.
"You're the first": Williams, *To the Angels*, 220.

Margaret Utinsky

"The men of Corregidor": Utinsky, *Miss U: Angel of the Underground*, 10.
Statistics for the Bataan Death March: Bill Sloan. *Undefeated: America's Heroic Fight for Bataan and Corregidor* (New York: Simon & Schuster, 2012), 183; John C. Shively, *Profiles in Survival: The Experiences of American POWs in the Philippines during World War II* (Indianapolis: Indiana Historical Society Press, 2012), 396.
"the hike": Lukacs, *Escape From Davao: The Forgotten Story of the Most Daring Prison Break of the Pacific War*, 73.
"I knew that": Utinsky, *Miss U*, 20.
"Risks did not": Utinsky, *Miss U*, 47.
"Dear Miss U": Utinsky, *Miss U*, 64.
"If he could have": Utinsky, *Miss U*, 64.
"Where is your gun?": Binkowski, *Code Name: High Pockets; True Story of Claire Phillips, an American Mata Hari and the WWII Resistance Movement in the Philippines*, 134.
"There are four": Binkowski, *High Pockets*, 137.
"You will come": Utinsky, *Miss U*, 91.

Yay Panlilio

"We to whom": Panlilio, *The Crucible: An Autobiography by Colonel Yay, Filipina American Guerrilla*, 13.
"the Major": Panlilio, *Crucible*, 17.
"War was our marriage": Panlilio, *Crucible*, 26.
"After the march": Binkowski, *Code Name: High Pockets; True Story of Claire Phillips, an American Mata Hari and the WWII Resistance Movement in the Philippines*, 42–43.

"The Marking Guerillas' Creed": Panlilio, *Crucible*, 3.

"You are the brain": Panlilio, *Crucible*, 23.

"We'll kill him . . . I love you": Panlilio, *Crucible*, 37.

"scarred by their own brutalities": Panlilio, *Crucible*, 50.

"I was a one-woman . . . fight to the end": Panlilio, *Crucible*, 61–62.

"To leave them": Panlilio, *Crucible*, 135.

"I don't need to be": Panlilio, *Crucible*, 155.

"Authorization means . . . relay the orders": Panlilio, *Crucible*, 155–156.

"wrenched . . . to every possible": Robert Lapham and Bernard Norling, *Lapham's Raiders. Lapham's Raiders: Guerillas in the Philippines* (Lexington: University Press of Kentucky, 1996), 194.

"Whereas, this organization": Panlilio, *Crucible*, 305.

"While 18,000 such claims": "Filipino World War II Veterans," White House Initiative on Asian Americans and Pacific Islanders, sites .ed.gov/aapi/filipino-world-war-ii-veterans/.

Claire Phillips

"Our new show . . . High Pockets": Claire and Goldsmith, *Manila Espionage*, 105.

"So why don't . . . one by one": Binkowski, *Code Name: High Pockets; True Story of Claire Phillips, an American Mata Hari and the WWII Resistance Movement in the Philippines*, 30.

"But I beg": Claire and Goldsmith, *Manila Espionage*, 104.

"You should have . . . repairs on submarines": Binkowski, *High Pockets*, 118.

"Heart sank . . . on their legs": Claire and Goldsmith, *Manila Espionage*, 125.

Repairmen, milkmen, meter readers: Binkowski, *High Pockets*, 99.

"Jitto shita cri! . . . High Pockets": Claire and Goldsmith, *Manila Espionage*, 172.

"I don't know": Binkowski, *High Pockets*, 161.

Maria Rosa Henson

"They should be": Henson, *Comfort Woman: A Filipina's Story of Prostitution and Slavery Under the Japanese Military*, 34.

"I am one": Henson, *Comfort Woman*, 34.

"*We looked at . . . kill us instantly*": Henson, *Comfort Woman*, 35.

"*I walked to*": Henson, *Comfort Woman*, 36.

"*hell*": Henson, *Comfort Woman*, 36.

approximately 200,000: Yoshiaki, *Comfort Women: Sexual Slavery in the Japanese Military During World War II*, 91–94.

Statistics on Filipina comfort women were taken from Henson, *Comfort Woman*, xii–xiii.

"*At the end*": Henson, *Comfort Woman*, 37.

"*I cried every night*": Henson, *Comfort Woman*, 41.

"*He could do*": Henson, *Comfort Woman*, 44.

"*Don't be ashamed . . . dirty and repulsive*": Henson, *Comfort Woman*, 83.

"*I felt like*": Henson, *Comfort Woman*, 85.

"*There were others*": Henson, *Comfort Woman*, 86.

a total of 168: Obituary of Maria Rosa Henson, *New York Times*, August 17, 1997.

"*learned to remember . . . will feel humiliated*": Obituary.

Excerpts from Henson, *Comfort Woman*, reprinted by permission of Rowman & Littlefield.

Sybil Kathigasu

"*Have you heard*": Kathigasu, *No Dram of Mercy*, 15.

"*It's the guerillas*": Kathigasu, *No Dram*, 60.

"*I could not approve*": Kathigasu, *No Dram*, 60.

"*Very well, Bil*": Kathigasu, *No Dram*, 70.

"*What are these for*": Kathigasu, *No Dram*, 75.

"*We cannot avoid*": Kathigasu, *No Dram*, 94.

"*there is comfort in that*": Kathigasu, *No Dram*, 105.

"*Speak!*": Kathigasu, *No Dram*, 180.

"*Don't tell, Mummy . . . Now I know that it is true*": Kathigasu, *No Dram*, 181.

"*Long live Malaya*": Kathigasu, *No Dram*, 182.

"*The Japanese capitulated*": Kathigasu, *No Dram*, 231.

Elizabeth Choy

All Elizabeth Choy quotations taken from her oral history interview, accession no. 597, used with permission from the Oral

History Centre, National Archives of Singapore, www.nas.gov.sg /archivesonline/oral_history_interviews/search-result?search -type=advanced&accessionNo=000597.

Elizabeth Choy . . . was never interested in politics: Zhou Mei, *Elizabeth Choy: More than a War Heroine,* (Singapore: Landmark Books, 1995), 58.

The worst disaster . . . advance planning: Rees, *Horror in the East,* 72.

Vivian Bullwinkel

Description of Singapore on February 12 comes from Betty Jeffrey, *White Coolies* (London: Angus and Robertson, 1954), 4.

"Take cover!": Manners, *Bullwinkel: The True Story of Vivian Bullwinkel, a Young Army Nursing Sister Who Was the Sole Survivor of a World War Two Massacre by the Japanese,* 66.

"These are the people": Manners, *Bullwinkel,* 79.

"Bully . . . it's true then": Manners, *Bullwinkel,* 80.

"in a strange and": Manners, *Bullwinkel,* 81.

"Chin up, girls": Manners, *Bullwinkel,* 81.

"So this is what": Manners, *Bullwinkel,* 81.

"I'm not dead": Manners, *Bullwinkel,* 81.

"Where have you been": Manners, *Bullwinkel,* 84.

"Please, just a": Manners, *Bullwinkel,* 92.

"If it comes to": Manners, *Bullwinkel,* 93.

"I want you to know . . . determined to be like you": Manners, *Bullwinkel,* 99.

"All these fine": Manners, *Bullwinkel,* 101.

Statistics on the Burma Railway come from The Thai-Burma Railway and Hellfire Pass, http://hellfire-pass.commemoration.gov. au/building-hellfire-pass/.

"They're all dead": Manners, *Bullwinkel,* 103.

"Sister . . . a little while longer": Manners, *Bullwinkel,* 109.

Excerpts from *Bullwinkel,* © 2008 Norman Manners, used by permission.

Helen Colijn

Helen's musings while grave digging are taken from Colijn, *Song of Survival: Women Interned,* 165–166.

An elderly Chinese man: Manners, *Bullwinkel: The True Story of Vivian Bullwinkel, a Young Army Nursing Sister Who Was the Sole Survivor of a World War Two Massacre by the Japanese,* 129–30.

"If this goes on for long": Colijn, *Song of Survival,* 128.

"Father, in captivity": Excerpts from *The Captives Hymn* used by permission of Betty Pryce-Jones.

"Everyone knows already . . . if you take the trouble": Colijn, *Song of Survival,* 132.

"Enjoy our surprise": Colijn, *Song of Survival,* 129.

"You must be going to that concert": Colijn, *Song of Survival,* 130–31.

"This evening": Colijn, *Song of Survival,* 135.

"The music soared": Colijn, *Song of Survival,* 136.

"Huu, huu": Colijn, *Song of Survival,* 136.

"looked oddly alone": Colijn, *Song of Survival,* 138.

"they had never seen": Colijn, *Song of Survival,* 190.

"never let a false": Colijn, *Song of Survival,* 146.

"When I sang that": Colijn, *Song of Survival,* 146.

Excerpts from Colijn, *Song of Survival* (White Cloud Press, 1995), used by permission of the publisher.

Jane Kendeigh

"had a bad feeling": Jane Kendeigh Cheverton family papers.

"Don't worry": Cheverton family papers.

"There's Iwo": DeWitt, *The First Navy Flight Nurse on a Pacific Battlefield: A Picture Story of a Flight to Iwo Jima,* n.p.

"bursting shells . . . Fourth of July": DeWitt, *First Navy Flight Nurse,* n.p.

"anxious": Sutter, "Angel of Mercy Kept Wings: WWII Nurse Still Dotes on Patients," *San Diego Union,* March 24, 1985.

"Were you frightened . . . breath came short": Page Cooper, *Navy Nurse,* (New York: McGraw-Hill, 1946), 174.

"You live on . . . through that": Sutter, "Angel of Mercy."

"Perhaps you're wondering": Sutter, "Angel of Mercy."

"It was so unexpected": Sutter, "Angel of Mercy."

"I had never seen": Rees, *Horror in the East,* 113.

"Now you just . . . hasn't changed a bit": Cheverton family papers.

Dickey Chapelle

"Are you a writer": Chapelle, *What's a Woman Doing Here? A Reporter's Report on Herself,* 64.

"Just be sure": Chapelle, *What's a Woman Doing Here?,* 63.

"You can't be both": Chapelle, *What's a Woman Doing Here?,* 65.

"Never heard of one": Chapelle, *What's a Woman Doing Here?,* 65

"There was not . . . Corps after this": Chapelle, *What's a Woman Doing Here?,* 66.

"I was certain . . . on Iwo Jima": Chapelle, *What's a Woman Doing Here?,* 66–67.

"Incomplete casualty reports": Chapelle, *What's a Woman Doing Here?,* 67.

"Poetic, isn't he": Chapelle, *What's a Woman Doing Here?,* 67.

"An unconfirmed rumor": Chapelle, *What's a Woman Doing Here?,* 68.

It has been": Chapelle, *What's a Woman Doing Here?,* 68.

"Now that I": Chapelle, *What's a Woman Doing Here?,* 68.

"A Japanese bomber": Chapelle, *What's a Woman Doing Here?,* 72.

"Shapeless dirty bloody": Chapelle, *What's a Woman Doing Here?,* 77.

"I—feel—lucky . . . guy feel lucky": Chapelle, *What's a Woman Doing Here?,* 78.

"After that, I": Chapelle, *What's a Woman Doing Here?,* 79.

"The situation was . . . Okay, okay—move!" Chapelle, *What's a Woman Doing Here?,* 84–85.

"We had a": Hastings, *Retribution: The Battle for Japan, 1944–1945,* 253.

"You don't have . . . about you now." Chapelle, *What's a Woman Doing Here?,* 89–90.

"Far forward as": Chapelle, *What's a Woman Doing Here?* 91.

"Tell me every . . . were not wasps": Chapelle, *What's a Woman Doing Here?,* 95.

"No experience in": Chapelle, *What's a Woman Doing Here?,* 123.

"Anybody would know": Chapelle, *What's a Woman Doing Here?,* 115.

"How can he . . . never been reached." Chapelle, *What's a Woman Doing Here?,* 116–117.

"The wounded looked": Ostroff, *Fire in the Wind: The Life of Dickey Chapelle,* 124.

"passed like wildfire": Meg Jones, "Legendary War Photographer Dickey Chapelle Back in Focus," October 17, 2014, *Milwaukee Journal Sen-*

tinel, www.jsonline.com/news/milwaukee/legendary-war-photo grapher-dickey-chapelle-back-in-focus-b99371912z1-279644882. html.

"she was one of us": Ostroff, *Fire in the Wind,* 390.

"be careful . . . with the marines": Ostroff, *Fire in the Wind,* 390.

Excerpts from *What's a Woman Doing Here?* © 1962 Dickey Chapelle, used by permission of the Meyer family.

Epilogue

70,000 Okinawan civilians: Spector, *Eagle Against the Sun: The American War with Japan,* 540.

over 300,000 Japanese civilians: Conversation with Robert Messer, professor emeritus, 20th-century history, University of Illinois at Chicago.

American code breakers . . . fight to the death: Frank, *Downfall: The End of the Imperial Japanese Empire,* 108; Spector, *Eagle,* 549.

Survivors of the fierce fighting: Various written testimony and the author's personal conversations with WWII veterans.

now included teenagers and old men: Hastings, *Retribution,* 439; 438, McCullough, *Truman.*

thousands of additional Purple Hearts: Allen and Polmar, *Codename Downfall,* 292; D. M. Giangreco and Kathryn Moore, "Half a Million Purple Hearts," *American Heritage,* 51, no. 8 (2000): 81.

would total 250,000: Frank, *Downfall,* 338, 340; McCullough, *Truman,* 437.

1,600,000 Soviet troops: Toland, *The Rising Sun: The Decline and Fall of the Japanese Empire, 1936–1945,* 986.

"prompt and utter destruction": Potsdam Declaration, Atomic Archive, www.atomicarchive.com/Docs/Hiroshima/Potsdam.shtml.

"an iron curtain": Winston S. Churchill, "Iron Curtain Speech," Fordham University, legacy.fordham.edu/halsall/mod/churchill-iron .asp.

43,000 Japanese soldiers: Frank, *Downfall,* 263.

21,000 and 40,000: John R. Bruning, *Bombs Away! The World War II Bombing Campaigns over Europe,* (Minneapolis: Zenith, 2011), 275.

Truman quote issued on the day of the Hiroshima attack, taken from Harry S. Truman Library and Museum website, paper no. 93,

"Statement by the President Announcing the Use of the A-Bomb at Hiroshima," http://trumanlibrary.org/publicpapers/index.php?pid =100.

world opinion: Frank, *Downfall*, 270.

"There is really no . . . odds against us!": Toland, *Rising Sun*, 1000.

"only had to endure . . . like a monster": Cook, *Japan at War: An Oral History*, 384–386.

"I cannot bear . . . bear the unbearable": Toland, *The Rising Sun*, 1005–1006.

"out of Our . . . human civilization": Cook, *Japan at War*, 401.

natural disaster: Cook, *Japan at War*, 406.

Approximately 1,000 war criminals: John W. Dower, *Embracing Defeat: Japan in the Wake of World War II* (New York: W. W. Norton, 1999), 447; Kazuko Tsurumi, *Social Change and the Individual* (Princeton, NJ: Princeton University Press, 1970), 139; Laura Hillenbrand, *Unbroken: A World War II Story of Survival, Resilience, and Redemption* (New York: Random House, 2010), 335.

approximately six million: R. J. Rummel, "Statistics of Japanese Democide Estimates, Calculations, and Sources," www.hawaii.edu /powerkills/SOD.CHAP3.HTM.

BIBLIOGRAPHY

Those titles marked with an asterisk are particularly suited to younger readers.

Books

Allen, Thomas B., and Norman Polmar. *Code-Name Downfall: The Secret Plan to Invade Japan and Why Truman Dropped the Bomb.* New York: Simon & Schuster, 1995.

* Atwood, Kathryn J. *Women Heroes of World War II: 26 Stories of Espionage, Sabotage, Resistance, and Rescue.* Chicago: Chicago Review Press, 2011.

Aylward, Gladys. *The Little Woman.* Chicago: Moody, 1970.

Benjamin, Robert Spiers, ed. *Eye Witness by Members of the Overseas Press Club of America.* New York: Alliance Book Corporation, 1940.

Binkowski, Edna Bautista. *Code Name: High Pockets; True Story of Claire Phillips, an American Mata Hari and the WWII Resistance Movement in the Philippines.* Limay, Bataan: Valour, 2006.

Bitton-Jackson, Livia. *I Have Lived a Thousand Years: Growing Up in the Holocaust.* New York: Simon Pulse, 1997.

Breu, Mary. *Last Letters from Attu: The True Story of Etta Jones, Alaska Pioneer and Japanese P.O.W.* Portland, OR: Graphic Arts Books, 2009.

Burgess, Alan. *The Small Woman: The Heroic Story of Gladys Aylward.* London: Reprint Society, 1957.

* Caravantes, Peggy. *The Many Faces of Josephine Baker: Dancer, Singer, Activist, Spy.* Chicago Review Press, 2015.

Chang, Iris. *The Rape of Nanking: The Forgotten Holocaust of World War II.* New York: Penguin, 1998.

Chapelle, Dickey. *What's a Woman Doing Here? A Reporter's Report on Herself.* New York: William Morrow, 1962.

Colijn, Helen. *Song of Survival: Women Interned.* Ashland, OR: White Cloud Press, 1995.

*Colman, Penny. *Adventurous Women: Eight True Stories About Women Who Made a Difference.* New York: Henry Holt, 2006.

Cook, Haruko Taya and Theodore F. *Japan at War: An Oral History.* New York: New Press, 1992.

* DeWitt, Lieutenant Gill, USN. *The First Navy Flight Nurse on a Pacific Battlefield: A Picture Story of a Flight to Iwo Jima.* Fredricksburg, TX: The Admiral Nimitz Foundation, 1983.

Dower, John W. *Embracing Defeat: Japan in the Wake of World War II.* New York: W. W. Norton, 1999.

*Farrell, Mary Cronk. *Pure Grit: How American World War II Nurses Survived Battle and Prison Camp in the Pacific.* New York: Abrams Books for Young Readers, 2014.

Felton, Mark. *The Real Tenko: Extraordinary True Stories of Women Prisoners of the Japanese.* Barnsley, South Yorkshire: Pen & Sword Books, 2009.

Frank, Richard B. *Downfall: The End of the Imperial Japanese Empire.* New York: Random House, 1999.

Garofolo, John. *Dickey Chapelle Under Fire: Photographs by the First American Female War Correspondent Killed in Action.* Madison, WI: Wisconsin Historical Society Press, 2015.

Harmsen, Peter. *Shanghai 1937: Stalingrad on the Yangtze.* Philadelphia: Casemate, 2013.

Hastings, Max. *Retribution: The Battle for Japan, 1944–1945.* New York: Alfred A. Knopf, 2008.

Henson, Maria Rosa. *Comfort Woman: A Filipina's Story of Prostitution and Slavery Under the Japanese Military*. Lanham, MD: Rowman & Littlefield, 1999.

* Hillenbrand, Laura. *Unbroken (The Young Adult Adaptation): An Olympian's Journey from Airman to Castaway to Captive*. New York: Delacort, 2014.

* Hollihan, Kerrie Logan. *Reporting Under Fire: 16 Daring Women War Correspondents and Photojournalists*. Chicago: Chicago Review Press, 2014.

Hotta, Eri. *Japan 1941: Countdown to Infamy*. New York: Alfred A. Knopf, 2013.

Houston, Jeanne Wakatsuki, and James D. Houston. *Farewell to Manzanar*. Boston: Houghton Mifflin, 1973.

Hu, Hua-ling. *American Goddess at the Rape of Nanking: The Courage of Minnie Vautrin*. Carbondale and Edwardsville: Southern Illinois University Press, 2000.

Hu, Hua-ling and Zhang Lian-hong, eds. *The Undaunted Women of Nanking: The Wartime Diaries of Minnie Vautrin and Tsen Shui-Fang*. Carbondale and Edwardsville: Southern Illinois University Press, 2010.

Ishigaki, Ayako. *Restless Wave: My Life in Two Words: A Memoir*. New York: Feminist Press at the City University of New York, 2004.

Kaminski, Theresa. *Angels of the Underground: The American Women who Resisted the Japanese in the Philippines in World War II*. New York: Oxford, 2016.

Kaminski, Theresa. *Prisoners in Paradise: American Women in the Wartime South Pacific*. Lawrence: University Press of Kansas, 2000.

Kathigasu, Sybil. *No Dram of Mercy*. Singapore: Oxford University Press, 1983.

Kathigasu, Sybil, Chin Peng, Norma Miraflor, and Ian Ward. *Faces of Courage: A Revealing Historical Appreciation of Colonial Malaya's Legendary Kathigasu Family*. Singapore: Media Masters, 2006.

Kelly, Clara Olink. *The Flamboya Tree: A Family's War-Time Courage*. London: Arrow Books, 2002.

Knox, Donald. *Death March: The Survivors of Bataan*. New York: Harcourt Brace Jovanovich, 1981.

Krancher, Jan A. *The Defining Years of the Dutch East Indies 1942–1949: Survivors Accounts of Japanese Invasion and Enslavement of Europeans and the Revolution That Created Free Indonesia.* Jefferson, NC: McFarland, 1996.

Li, Peter, ed. *Japanese War Crimes: The Search for Justice.* Piscataway, NJ: Transaction, 2003.

Lukacs, John D. *Escape From Davao: The Forgotten Story of the Most Daring Prison Break of the Pacific War.* New York: New American Library, 2011.

MacDonald, Elizabeth P. *Undercover Girl.* New York: MacMillan, 1947.

Manners, Norman G. *Bullwinkel: The True Story of Vivian Bullwinkel, a Young Army Nursing Sister Who Was the Sole Survivor of a World War Two Massacre by the Japanese.* Western Australia: Hesperian, 2008.

Matsuda, Mary Gruenewald. *Looking Like the Enemy: My Story of Imprisonment in Japanese-American Internment Camps (The Young Reader's Edition).* Troutdale, OR: NewSage, 2010.

McCullough, David. *Truman.* New York: Simon & Schuster, 1993.

Mitter, Rana. *Forgotten Ally: China's World War II: 1937–1945.* Boston: Houghton Mifflin Harcourt, 2013.

Norman, Elizabeth M. *We Band of Angels: The Untold Story of American Nurses Trapped on Bataan by the Japanese.* New York: Simon & Schuster, 1999.

*Oppenheim, Joanne. *Dear Miss Breed: True Stories of the Japanese American Incarceration During World War II and a Librarian Who Made a Difference.* New York: Scholastic, 2006.

* Overy, Richard. *War in the Pacific.* New York: Osprey Publishing, 2010.

Ostroff, Roberta. *Fire in the Wind: The Life of Dickey Chapelle.* Annapolis: Bluejacket Books, 1992.

Panlilio, Yay. *The Crucible: An Autobiography by Colonel Yay, Filipina American Guerrilla.* New Brunswick, NJ: Rutgers University Press, 2009.

Phillips, Claire ("High Pockets"), and Myron B. Goldsmith. *Manila Espionage.* Hillsboro, OR: Binfords & Mort, 1947.

Prange, Gordon W. *Target Tokyo: The Story of the Sorge Spy Ring.* New York: McGraw-Hill, 1984.

Ramsey, Edwin Price, and Stephen J. Rivele. *Lieutenant Ramsey's War: From Horse Soldier to Guerrilla Commander.* New York: Knightsbridge, 1990.

Read, Dorothy and Ilse Evelijn Veere Smit. *End the Silence.* Greenbank, WA: Double-Isle, 2011.

Rees, Laurence. *Horror in the East.* London: BBC Worldwide, Ltd., 2001.

Rodriggs, Lawrence Reginald. *We Remember Pearl Harbor: Honolulu Civilians Recall the War Years, 1941–1945.* Newark, CA: Communications Concepts, 1991.

Romulo, Carlos P. *I Saw the Fall of the Philippines.* Garden City, NY: Doubleday, 1944.

Romulo, Carlos P. *I See the Philippines Rise.* Garden City, NY: Doubleday, 1946.

Ruff-O'Herne, Jan. *Fifty Years of Silence: Comfort Woman of Indonesia.* Sydney: Editions Tom Thompson, 1994.

Shaw, Ian W. *On Radji Beach: The Story of the Australian Nurses After the Fall of Singapore.* Sydney: MacMillan Australia, 2010.

* Sheinkin, Steve. *Bomb: The Race to Build—and Steal—the World's Most Dangerous Weapon.* New York: Roaring Books Press, 2012.

Sides, Hampton. *Ghost Soldiers: The Epic Account of World War II's Greatest Rescue Mission.* New York: Random House, 2001.

Smith, Colin. *Singapore Burning: Heroism and Surrender in World War II.* London: Penguin Books, 2005.

Smith, Wilda M. and Eleanor A. Bogart. *The Wars of Peggy Hull: The Life and Times of a War Correspondent.* El Paso: Texas Western Press, 1991.

Spector, Ronald H. *Eagle Against the Sun: The American War with Japan.* New York: Free Press, 1985.

Toland, John. *The Rising Sun: The Decline and Fall of the Japanese Empire, 1936–1945.* 2 vols. New York: Random House, 1970.

Utinsky, Margaret. *Miss U.* San Antonio, TX: Naylor, 1948.

Weinberg, Gerhard L. *A World at Arms: A Global History of World War II.* Cambridge: Cambridge University Press, 2005.

Williams, Denny. *To the Angels.* San Francisco: Denson, 1985.

Yoshiaki, Yoshimi. *Comfort Women: Sexual Slavery in the Japanese Military During World War II.* Translated by Suzanne O'Brien. New York: Columbia University Press, 1995.

Zamperini, Louis, with David Rensin. *Devil at My Heels: A Heroic Olympian's Astonishing Story of Survival as a Japanese POW in World War II*. New York: Harper Collins, 2003.

Zich, Arthur. *The Rising Sun*. Pueblo, CO: Time Life Books, 1977.

Collections

Chapelle, Dickey. Papers. Wisconsin Historical Society.

Choy, Elizabeth. Interview, accession number 597. Oral History Centre, National Archives of Singapore. www.nas.gov.sg/archives online/oral_history_interviews/search-result?search-type =advanced&accessionNo=000597.

Harry S. Truman Library and Museum. www.trumanlibrary.org.

Kendeigh, Jane. Papers. Private family collection.

Vautrin, Minnie. Papers. Yale Divinity School Library.

Online articles

"Comparing the American Inter[n]ment of Japanese-, German-, and Italian-Americans During World War II." Institute for Research of Expelled Germans. http://expelledgermans.org/germaninternment.htm.

"MacArthur's Speeches." American Experience. www.pbs.org/wgbh /amex/macarthur/filmmore/reference/primary/macspeech02 .html.

Senatore, Holly. "Bushido: The Valor of Deceit." *Military History Online*. www.militaryhistoryonline.com/wwii/articles/bushido.aspx.

Sobocinski, Andre. "Angels of the Airfields: Navy Air Evacuation Nurses of World War II." Naval Historical Foundation. www.navy history.org/2013/05/angels-of-the-airfields-navy-air-evacuation -nurses-ww2/.

Newspaper Articles

Sutter, Janet. "Angel of Mercy Kept Wings: WWII Nurse Still Dotes on Patients." *San Diego Union*, March 24, 1985.

INDEX